CAMBRIDGE MUSIC HANDBOOKS

Sibelius: Symphony No. 5

CAMBRIDGE MUSIC HANDBOOKS

GENERAL EDITOR Julian Rushton

Cambridge Music Handbooks provide accessible introductions to major musical works, written by the most informed commentators in the field.

With the concert-goer, performer and student in mind, the books present essential information on the historical and musical context, the composition, and the performance and reception history of each work, or group of works, as well as critical discussion of the music.

Other published titles

Bach: Mass in B Minor JOHN BUTT
Beethoven: *Missa solemnis* WILLIAM DRABKIN
Berg: Violin Concerto ANTHONY POPLE
Chopin: The Four Ballades JIM SAMSON
Handel: *Messiah* DONALD BURROWS
Haydn: *The Creation* NICHOLAS TEMPERLEY
Haydn: String Quartets, Op. 50 W. DEAN SUTCLIFFE
Janáček: *Glagolitic Mass* PAUL WINGFIELD
Mahler: Symphony No. 3 PETER FRANKLIN
Musorgsky: *Pictures at an Exhibition* MICHAEL RUSS
Schoenberg: *Pierrot lunaire* JONATHAN DUNSBY
Schubert: *Die schöne Müllerin* SUSAN YOUENS
Schumann: Fantasie, Op. 17 NICHOLAS MARSTON

Sibelius: Symphony No. 5

James Hepokoski

Professor of Musicology, University of Minnesota

Published by the Press Syndicate of the University of Cambridge
The Pitt Building, Trumpington Street, Cambridge CB2 1RP
40 West 20th Street, New York, NY 10011–4211, USA
10 Stamford Road, Oakleigh, Victoria 3166, Australia

First published 1993

Printed in Great Britain at the University Press, Cambridge

A cataloguing in publication record for this book is available from the British Library

Library of Congress cataloguing in publication data

Hepokoski, James A. (James Arnold), 1946–
Sibelius, Symphony no. 5 / James Hepokoski.
p. cm. – (Cambridge music handbooks)
Includes bibliographical references and index.
ISBN 0 521 40143 7 (hardback) – ISBN 0 521 40958 6 (paperback)
I. Sibelius, Jean, 1865–1957. Symphonies, no. 5, op. 82, E♭ major.
I. Title. II. Series.
ML410.S54H4 1993
784.2'184–dc20 91–21614 CIP MN

ISBN 0 521 40143 7 hardback
ISBN 0 521 40958 6 paperback

AH

for Joanna and Laura

  . . . Hark! the rushing snow!
The sun-awakened avalanche! whose mass,
Thrice sifted by the storm, had gathered there
Flake after flake, in heaven-defying minds
As thought by thought is piled, till some great truth
Is loosened, and the nations echo round,
Shaken to their roots, as do the mountains now.

Shelley, *Prometheus Unbound*, II.iii

Art then is the becoming and happening of truth. . . . Truth is never gathered from objects that are present and ordinary. Rather, the opening up of the Open, and the clearing of what is, happens only as the openness is projected, sketched out, that makes its advent in thrownness. . . . Poetry, however, is not an aimless imagining of whimsicalities and not a flight of mere notions and fancies into the realm of the unreal. What poetry, as illuminating projection, unfolds of unconcealedness and projects ahead into the design of the figure, is the Open which poetry lets happen, and indeed in such a way that only now, in the midst of beings, the Open brings beings to shine and ring out. . . .

Heidegger, *The Origin of the Work of Art* (71–2)

  Today at ten to eleven I saw 16 swans. One of my
greatest experiences. Lord God, that beauty!

Sibelius, Diary, 21 April 1915

Contents

Preface

It is rather impossible to explain art with words, therefore I don't like to speak about my music. When I do I regret it the next day. The listener has unlimited possibilities of misunderstanding me and limited possibilities of understanding me.[1]

A good threshold: Sibelius's words stand as a warning to commentators on his music. And they are reinforced by the current state of hermeneutics and critical theory, which would regard as naive any claim, implicit or explicit, to have objectively understood the workings of any cultural artifact, much less such a multifaceted and socio-aesthetically complex one as the Fifth Symphony. What follows here, then, reflects only the current state of my own dialogue with that work and the material and psychological conditions under which it arose – a dialogue with which I confess to having been fascinated for as long as I can remember.

Sibelius's work on the Fifth Symphony's three performed versions from summer 1914 to its eventual publication by Wilhelm Hansen in 1921 forms an enormously complex story that cannot be offered in full detail here. Merely to compare the three versions adequately would exceed the space allotted, but we are also confronted with numerous sketches, drafts, partial revisions, diary entries, letters, and the like. Moreover, the concurrent European political dimension deserves a far more thorough treatment than the reader will find here. Dominated by world-war politics (and, for Finland, a politics crowned with independence on 6 December 1917 from Russia, but followed immediately by a fierce civil war between the Marxist-oriented 'Reds' and the liberal-democratic 'Whites'), these years occupy the entire fourth volume of Tawaststjerna's indispensable Sibelius biography: some 414 pages.[2]

Particularly since Tawaststjerna's final volumes (4 and 5) will be available in Robert Layton's English translation before too long, it seemed redundant merely to summarize or duplicate the information in that work. The only reason to write any book (and certainly this one) is to offer perspectives on a topic that are unavailable elsewhere. Consequently, my aim has been to furnish something of a reflective, complementary commentary to Tawaststjerna and frankly to refer the reader interested in more details – and in more biographical and 'humanizing' byways – to that book. Particularly with regard to the Fifth's genesis, my more limited purpose will be twofold: to provide an essential summary of what seem to me to be the most significant aspects of Sibelius's symphonic concerns during these years; and, in the process, to bring to light certain aspects of the source materials that Tawaststjerna did not discuss.

More broadly, my larger aim is to challenge and redefine the categories under which Sibelius's music is perceived. With regard to the Fifth Symphony this is possible, I think, only by historicizing his work within the context of the principal musical clash of his times – the apparent shipwrecking of the liberal-bourgeois 'modernist' tradition against the more radical 'New Music' experiments of a younger generation. In confronting Sibelius, whose work is deliciously unclassifiable, the central battle has been for the definition of the reception framework. As such this century's Sibelius controversy has been shot through with the strident claims and counter-claims of our central aesthetic-political ideologies. Thus we have heard much (too much) of Sibelius the 'nationalist'; the 'exotic'; the 'conservative'; the composer – according to Cecil Gray – whose symphonies 'represent the highest point attained in this form since the death of Beethoven';[3] or, on the other hand – as proposed by Adorno, appalled by the 'culture industry's' embrace of Sibelius in the 1930s and 1940s – the composer whose 'symphonies combined meaningless and trivial elements with alogical and profoundly unintelligible ones', the composer who 'mistook esthetic formlessness for the voice of nature'.[4] These inappropriate – though seemingly ineradicable – positions have by now so muddied the Sibelius waters that one wonders whether any attempt to reconfront these works in less prejudicial terms is even possible in our times. This book is a modest attempt to try.

In writing it I am deeply indebted to many friends, colleagues, and fellow scholars. During my trips to Finland (made possible by grants from Oberlin College and the University of Minnesota) Professor Eero Tarasti and Kari Kilpeläinen, both of the University of Helsinki, along with Professor Fabian Dahlström of the Sibelius Museum in Turku, provided me with cascades of invaluable information and direct help at a time when all of it was totally new to me. At the Helsinki University Library, Laila Koukku generously facilitated my access to the precious Sibelius collection and assisted my work for weeks on end, and Helena Ahonen of the Helsinki City Orchestra Archives kindly supplied me with photocopies of some of the surviving materials for the 1916 version. I am also grateful to the Sibelius family who, through Mr Errki Virkkunen and with the assistance of Laila Koukku, granted me permission to reproduce my transcriptions of some of the sketches and 1915-version materials. All transcriptions from the final version of the symphony are made with the kind permission of the Wilhelm Hansen publishing firm in Copenhagen. Permission to transcribe materials from Sibelius's 1914–15 sketchbook was generously granted by the Estate of Jean Sibelius and the Otava Publishing Company, Ltd., Helsinki; in addition, the cover photograph is also reproduced courtesy of Otava. I should also like to thank several individuals who have taken an interest in this project and have helped me in a variety of ways: Tomi Mäkelä, Veijo Murtomäki, Erkki Salmenhaara, Glenda Dawn Goss, Warren Darcy, Paul Mast, and Richard Wattenbarger.

Concerning the translations that appear in this book, it is a pleasure to acknowledge the help of Timo Riippa, who guided me ably through portions of the fourth volume of Tawaststjerna's Finnish-language Sibelius biography. Without his help I could not have presented the Fifth Symphony's 'story' as fully (or as confidently) as I do here. I am also pleased to cite the assistance of Sari Rönnholm, who helped me through the final nuances of each translated sentence in this book, although I alone am responsible for any infelicities that remain. But I must conclude by emphasizing once again that all Sibelians owe their primary debt of thanks to the research of Erik Tawaststjerna, and alongside that research English speakers may also gratefully acknowledge the work of his translator (and ardent Sibelius champion for so many years), Robert Layton.

Introduction: Sibelius and the problem of 'modernism'

It is customary for historians to draw a line between Sibelius's dissonant, austere Fourth Symphony (1911) and the seemingly more accessible, comfortable Fifth (whose three versions received their premieres in 1915, 1916, and 1919). The gap often alleged to separate the two symphonies is that dividing the spirit of artistic 'progress' in the earlier work from its presumed absence in the later. However simplistic, the line has served to divide a generally legitimate earlier Sibelius, whose works may be approached without apology (especially the earlier ones, which can be conveniently, though reductively, collapsed into the somewhat tainted category of 'nationalism'), from a problematic, post-Fourth Symphony composer, whose idiosyncratic works clung to an eclipsed symphonic tradition in markedly anti-Romantic times.

Commentators have consequently embraced the Fourth Symphony, which in its uncompromising stance has traditionally been considered the most forward-looking of Sibelius's seven. The Fifth's more overt orchestral effects, triumphant conclusion, and popular appeal have required a bit of dodging, even for champions of the later works. 'The fifth symphony, with its imposing finale and heroic proportions', wrote Constant Lambert in 1934, 'might at first sight seem to be a mature reversion to an earlier mood, and it may be described as the most obviously great of Sibelius' symphonies. Actually, though, it is not a backward step but a gradual approach to the one monumental movement of No. 7.'[1] In such a scheme the Fifth, while subtly mixing progressive and regressive elements, is reduced to a way-station on the path to worthier things: the last two symphonies and *Tapiola*. Equally common, though, has been the suggestion that serious historians, if they are to bother with Sibelius at all, need not trouble themselves with the post-1911 works. Thus Carl Dahlhaus, writing sympathetically in 1980 of the Fourth: '[Here] Sibelius reached a "state of [the] musical material" (to borrow a phrase from his detractor, Adorno) which he was never to surpass, not even in his Seventh Symphony

(1924).'[2] Dahlhaus's point is nothing less than that after the Fourth Symphony Sibelius's music no longer belongs to 'history'.

In short, in many of the standard historical accounts the Fifth Symphony is Sibelius's *Der Rosenkavalier*, as the Fourth had been his *Elektra*. And just as has been the case with Strauss, it has been our assessment of the later work that has determined the main lines of our reconstruction of his career's trajectory: we tend both to retroject back and to project forward from the implications of the Fifth. It is the Fifth, then, not the Fourth, that occupies the pivotal point in Sibelius's output. Not surprisingly, of the completed symphonies it is the one over whose final shape he seems most to have struggled. (I except here the much-discussed Eighth Symphony, on which he apparently laboured from late 1926 through at least 1933 or 1934 – but then withheld and ultimately, it seems, destroyed by fire in the 1940s.)[3]

But again, as with Strauss, the Fifth's centrality to the Sibelius *œuvre* invites us to ponder difficult historical problems. Chief among them is that of a notable, *engagé* composer facing, but then apparently renouncing, the most advanced 'state of the musical material' of his time. By the period of the Fifth Symphony this included, most prominently, the aggressive 'emancipation of the dissonance'. Considered more broadly, the larger challenge was the attempt by younger radicals to delegitimize the expressive worlds that had been supported by the musical systems of Western European bourgeois liberalism for the past several decades. The socio-aesthetic dynamics at issue here are far-reaching in their implications. In order to perceive them we need to view more expansively the workings of a complex aesthetic institution.

Sibelius's output is best viewed as a significant constituent of a larger 'modern' wave of European composers born around 1860, a generational wave that included Elgar (1857), Puccini (1858), Mahler (1860), Wolf (1860), Debussy (1862), Strauss (1864), Sibelius (1865), Glazunov (1865), Nielsen (1865), Busoni (1866), and several others. Our key category of understanding at the outset, then, is that of a self-conscious 'musical modernism', which, as Dahlhaus has repeatedly argued, flourished 'between 1889 and 1914 as a self-contained period in music history'. The modern style initially defined itself as something youth-oriented and new, as something signalled by 'the breakaway mood of the 1890s (a mood symbolized musically by the opening bars of Strauss's *Don Juan*) . . . a fresh start in a new direction'.[4] Musicians at the turn of the century were much absorbed with the challenges posed by 'the moderns', and their own descriptions of the movement – frequently grounded in their assessments of Richard Strauss – ranged from Hans Merian's view that its essential feature lay in the liberation away from the architectonic in favour of ever more precise, colouristic effects to Oscar Bie's contention that modern music displayed an increased 'materialism', in which musical ideas were now spawned out of the implications of the technical material itself, instead of, as earlier, out of the reservoir of the human spirit.[5]

However we might choose to define this modernism, it is clear that the musical world that Sibelius's generation greeted differed significantly from that of its predecessors. This was the first generation to come of age in a post-Lisztian/post-Wagnerian world of recently reified or crystallized musical systems, whose very security and success could be understood to stand for a liberal, urbanized, and capitalistic Europe now nearing the crest of its own self-assurance. These in-place musical systems were the undisputed brokers of aesthetic power. We may regard them as coordinated on a broader level to constitute the epoch's 'institution of art music'.[6] They included fully-fledged, efficiently organized concert, recital, and operatic delivery systems supported by a network of entrepreneurs, performers, publishers, reviewers and critics, historians, educators, textbook-codified *Formenlehre* systems for composers to use as foils and points of reference, a fixed canon of past masterworks, and so on.

The 1889–1914 modernists sought to shape the earlier stages of their careers as individualistic seekers after the musically 'new', the bold, the controversial, and the idiosyncratic in structure and colour. But simultaneously, as sharp competitors in a limited marketplace, they were also eager to attract and then perpetuate the constituent parts of the delivery system. With few exceptions (the earlier Debussy may be one) their goal was to effect a relatively comfortable marriage between art and high-technology business. Within the *de facto* institution one strove to flourish as provocatively or enticingly as possible – to create an identifiable, personalized style that, while unmistakably emanating the aura, traditions, and high seriousness of 'art', also produced readily marketable commodities marked with an appropriately challenging, up-to-the-minute spice, boldness, or 'philosophical tone'. In short, one was encouraged to push the system to its socio-aesthetic limits, but not beyond them, as would be the case with the younger radicals.

Within the format of symphonic composition, Strauss, Mahler, and Sibelius number among this generation's major figures. From Sibelius's perspective the first two, as products of Austro-Germanic training and culture – 'native speakers', as it were – would have been more or less insiders, that is, active participants situated in social positions of non-ignorable prestige, power, and influence. (Admittedly, the actual situation was more complex, particularly when we consider such other aspects of social and racial tension as may be found, for example, in the reception of Mahler's career. Still, the point at hand is that, whatever the musical or personal judgments of individual contemporary critics and historians might have been, they rarely questioned Strauss's or Mahler's basic right of entry into the centre of symphonic discourse: one was obliged to take a stand on them, whether pro or con.)[7] Sibelius, correctly enough, saw himself viewed as an outsider, as a composer who from the Germanic cultural-political perspective was patronizable – or could be ignored entirely – as 'not one of us'. Walter Niemann's emphatic, if not phobic, dismissal of Sibelius's symphonies in 1917 was, among other things, a priestlike gesture within the cultic institution intended to keep pure the sacred space of Germanic symphonism. Thus Sibelius's symphonies were merely 'Northern': their thematic essence was foreign to 'a symphonic treatment in our sense . . . [that of] true symphonic creation – monumentality and closure of form, organic and logical development and shaping'; they impressed one as struggles over 'the imitation, perhaps, of Tchaikovsky's *Pathétique* in a Finnish dialect'; moreover, 'from the first to the last [symphony], their content is the same: Finland's soul in its nature and people'.[8] This fundamental cultural otherness shaped the reception of Sibelius's music on the continent. But from a broader perspective all three – doubtless along with Elgar, and probably Nielsen and Glazunov as well – should be considered the principal symphonic representatives of a generation that faced the same kinds of compositional and institutional challenges, however their individual solutions might have differed.

In the most general terms, the compositional careers of most of the moderns may be divided into two phases. The first, the active or competitive phase, is characterized by the forging of differently accented, individualized languages from the mid 1880s through, roughly, the first decade of the twentieth century. For each composer this was a phase of personal stylization to be defined through a persistent, aggressive stretching of established compositional norms. Because of the premium placed on originality, the moderns were hesitant to lapse into an unconsidered reliance on 'default' structural, melodic, or harmonic gestures. Thus, forging a personalized but marketable style around 1900 was a complicated, risky business. Such canon- and textbook-consecrated gestures as melodic simplicity, squarely periodic phrasing, frequent cadences and balanced resolutions, symmetrical recapitulations, essentially unaltered repetitions of phrases or sections, and harmonic, tonal, structural, or orchestral orthodoxy needed to be handled with great care. An overuse, or even a misplaced use, of such defaults (one that could strike the listener as aesthetically unaware of its own datedness) opened one to the charge of merely perpetuating an inconsequential epigonism. On the other hand, within the modern style it was entirely legitimate, and quite normal, to evoke traditional or antiquated gestures in a non-immediate way. For example, an 'old-world' melody or turn of phrase could be set forth 'as if in quotation marks' or as a retrospective evocation of a not-quite-graspable, naive, or pre-modern wholeness remembered or dreamt of, but now fading rapidly or inaccessible in current times. (Although their individual styles and intentions differed markedly, Mahler and Elgar, in particular, would be attracted to this technique.)

Even entire structures could receive this quotation-mark treatment. A central feature of the modernist aesthetic game – one in which Sibelius was an eager player – was implicitly or fragmentarily to refer to the generic formal conventions, perhaps as lost gestures or the founding gestures of the game, but then to override them. By the last third of the nineteenth century there had arisen a whole arsenal of what I have termed 'deformations' of the *Formenlehre* (standard-textbook) structures.[9] Certain 'sonata-deformational' procedures became both common and readily recognizable. To perceive many modern works appropriately we should not try to take their measure with the obsolete 'sonata' gauge, as is often attempted, but rather to understand that they invoke familiar, 'post-sonata' generic subtypes that have undergone, in various combinations, the effects of differing deformational procedures. These structures cannot be said to 'be' sonatas in any strict sense: this would be grossly reductive, and in the consideration of any such work nuances are everything. Still, as part of the perceptual framework within which they ask to be understood, they do depend on the listener's prior knowledge of the *Formenlehre* 'sonata'. A significant part of their content, that is, is in dialogue with the generic expectations of the sonata, even when some of the most important features of those expectations are not realized.

By the later nineteenth century the most prominent deformational procedures seem to have stemmed from key works of Berlioz, Mendelssohn, Schumann, Liszt, and Wagner, although certain structures of Beethoven, Weber, Schubert, and Chopin were by no means irrelevant. Although an adequate discussion of late-century sonata deformations would lead us even further afield, it should be mentioned that the various types were shared by all of the symphonic modernists, who apparently played off each other's solutions. Some of the most common deformation-procedure families – and we should note once again that any single musical structure may combine aspects of two or more families – include:

1 *The breakthrough deformation.* Here an unforeseen inbreaking of a seemingly new (although normally motivically related) event in or at the close of the 'developmental space' radically redefines the character and course of the movement and typically renders a normative, largely symmetrical recapitulation invalid. The breakthrough principle is a notable member of a set of strategies that seek to avoid a potentially redundant recapitulation. Its roots go back to such things as the first-movement portion of Schumann's Fourth Symphony, whose developmental space, in effect, turns its back on the generically well-behaved exposition in ways that have profound consequences for the rest of the work. Clear examples within 'modern' works, which are generally more eruptive, may be drawn from the first movement and finale of Mahler's First Symphony, the second movement of Mahler's Fifth along with the first movement of his Eighth, and Strauss's *Don Juan* and *Death and Transfiguration*.[10] As we shall see, Sibelius alludes to the breakthrough principle in the Fifth Symphony's first movement.

2 *The introduction-coda frame.* This procedure gives the effect of subordinating 'sonata-activity' to the overriding contents of an encasing introduction and coda (whose identity may also intrude into certain inner sections of the 'sonata'). A common result is the furnishing of two levels of aesthetic presence, for example (as often in works with a 'national' turn), that of a fuller, more emphatic framing-reality – or even that of a metaphorically 'present' narrator – which unfolds a subordinate sonata-process that is eventually absorbed back into the original, fuller presence at its end. Wagner's Overture to *Tannhäuser* seems to have provided an influential example (one that also contains a notably sonata-deformational interior),[11] and the procedure also occurs in virtually model formats in the initial movements of Tchaikovsky's Second, Glazunov's Fourth, and Elgar's First Symphonies. Earlier, generally less developed examples include (in embryo) Mendelssohn's Overture to *A Midsummer Night's Dream* and (more emphatically) several overtures of Berlioz and the first movements of Schubert's Ninth and Mendelssohn's 'Scottish' Symphonies.[12] The finale of Brahms's First also shares affinities with this family, as does, on a somewhat reduced scale, the first movement of Dvořák's Eighth.

3 *Episodes within the developmental space.* Here the space normally allotted to development is partially or wholly given over to one or more – but often a pair of – episodes, which may or may not be motivically related to material

heard earlier. Developmental spaces with interpolated single episodes may be found in Weber's *Euryanthe* Overture, Wagner's *Tannhäuser* Overture, and Brahms's *Tragic* Overture. More thoroughgoing instances feature two episodes that extend over most of the developmental space, as in Berlioz's *Les franc-juges* Overture (possibly),[13] Liszt's *Tasso*, Wagner's *Siegfried Idyll*, and, within the 'modern' style, several of Strauss's symphonic poems, including *Macbeth*, *Don Juan*, and *Death and Transfiguration*.[14]

4 *Various strophic/sonata hybrids*. These occur occasionally in Mahler: the finale of the *Resurrection* Symphony (three broad, multithematic strophes simultaneously articulating a sonata deformation, or vice-versa) and the opening and closing movements of *Das Lied von der Erde* spring to mind. The Sibelian process that I shall identify in chapters 3–5 below as 'rotational form' is a member of this general family of deformational procedures. Perhaps significantly, some of the clearest precedents – including the first movement of Beethoven's *Appassionata* Sonata and the finale of Mendelssohn's 'Scottish' Symphony (both with 'four strophes' of a first/second theme-pattern) – are also early examples of 'formal' sonata movements that lack the important expositional repeat. (Within orchestral, non-concerto genres early in the century, the expositional repeat was to be omitted in operatic or concert overtures, but not in symphonies.) In addition, several idiosyncratic early fusions of the strophic and sonata principles are to be found in Berlioz: in the second portion of the first movement of *Harold in Italy*, for instance, or in the invigoratingly anarchic (and indeed quintessentially carnivalesque) overture, *Le Carnaval Romain*.[15]

5 *Multimovement forms in a single movement*, as so often in Liszt, Strauss, Schoenberg, and middle and late Sibelius. (See chapter 3 below, 'Interrelation and fusion of movements'.) Obvious sources earlier in the century are Schubert's *Wanderer Fantasy* and Schumann's Fourth Symphony. Wagner's Overture to *Die Meistersinger* has also been claimed as a compact precedent.[16]

These deformational procedures – along with several others[17] – are readily perceivable as norms within the first, active phase of liberal-bourgeois modernism. The second phase retains them, but its general expressive tone is now one either of disillusioned withdrawal from the 'progressive' marketplace or of the last-ditch – but doomed – defence of a beleaguered fortress. For each modernist the second phase was initiated by a personal confrontation with the more radical musical challenges of the years 1907–14, led mostly by two younger figures, one from the 1870s, Schoenberg, the other from the 1880s, Stravinsky. These were years in which the landscape of the institution of art music was undergoing nothing short of an earthquake. Suddenly outflanked, each of the moderns (particularly the symphonic or Germanic-oriented group) felt the ground slipping from under his feet. Within a few years an unforeseen historical twist – the onset of the New Music from a younger generation – was turning what had been perceived as aggressively modern into something faded and *passé*, something too snugly wedded to the old-world, liberal institutions of music and the aesthetically cultivated sectors of the middle class (*Bildungsbürgertum*) that they had sought to engage. The offence was suddenly put on the defence.

A mid-career decision was consequently forced upon each composer of the 1855–65 generation. And to a person, each declined to endorse – much less to embrace – the musical revolutions of Schoenberg and Stravinsky, even though each, quite accurately, perceived them as watershed events that brought the competitive phase of his own modern project to an end. Dahlhaus writes, for instance, of 'Strauss's and Reger's [ultimate] rejection of modernism . . . [which was] obviously influenced if not directly occasioned by the shock of Schönberg's earliest atonal compositions'.[18] As we shall see, Sibelius had precisely the same experience, and we would doubtless be obliged to think of Mahler in similar terms had he lived a decade or two longer: it hardly seems likely that he would have followed the Schoenberg School's lead into full atonality.

For each composer who survived into the second decade of the century, the withdrawal phase commonly involved a reflection on the nature of a grand but rapidly obsolescing musical language. We are thus presented with a charged dialectic of figure and ground that ought not to be resolved too hastily. On the one hand, the existing, in-place liberal-bourgeois institution of concert music provided the *de facto* framework of understanding – or ground – for the radical New Music (although this need not have been made explicit on that music's surface); on the other, the tacit presupposition of the now-withdrawing modernists was the presence of a new, aggressive musical language that was eclipsing their own. We might be encouraged, then, to listen to early atonal Schoenberg with the tonal, expressive, and structural horizons of expectation provided by the systems of liberal-bourgeois modernism. Conversely, we might listen to the post-1910 Sibelius, Strauss, Elgar, and so on, by realizing that these composers are deeply aware of using a language that does not bring to its acoustic surface the 'state of the musical material'. Nevertheless, that 'state of the material' does exist as a precondition of both musical production and reception: no composer can dismiss his or her aesthetic context by sheer fiat. Moreover, this awareness can be very much what such music is 'about'. In this deeper sense the 'state of the musical material' *is* present in such works, although it may not be foregrounded into explicit sound.

Broadly construed, this generational crisis is the foremost historical problem in which Sibelius and the Fifth Symphony are implicated. Our principal tasks will be to locate that work – and some of its immediate predecessors – within the tensions of the modernist/New Music confrontation, and then to inquire whether, and to what extent, we can uncover the historical content embedded in the language and structure of the Fifth Symphony itself.

2

The crisis, 1909–14: 'Let's let the world go its own way'

The Fifth Symphony is the first large-scale work that Sibelius composed fully on the other side of his confrontation with the New Music revolutions. Even more than the major works that immediately precede it, *The Bard* (1913, rev. 1914), *Luonnotar* (1913), and *The Oceanides* (1914), it marks his exit from a prolonged crisis of self-reappraisal, coupled with an uneasy acceptance of the withdrawal phase of his own modernism. Although he had entered the 1909–14 period with hopes of still contending publicly as a competing modernist, he left it resigned to failure, at least as judged by the marketplace terms of the institution of art music; resigned to a geographical and spiritual separation from the new currents of continental music; resigned to what he habitually called his *Alleingefühl* (sense of being alone, or total 'otherness'); and resigned, ultimately, to a solitary, interior journey of phenomenological concentration that seems to have had as its aim the uncovering of the hidden core, or 'being', of *Klang* (musical 'sound') itself.

One way to approach all of this is to underscore the degree to which the physical and psychological patterns of Sibelius's life in these years of change were split between two radically different modes of existence: the isolation of 'Ainola', his spare, idyllically rustic home in the forests of Järvenpää; and, in the sharpest possible contrast, his occasional visits to the grand capitals of European music, especially Berlin, Paris, and London. Thus on the one hand, Sibelius's life was one of utter retreat to a prolonged, solitary identification with an unspoiled nature; on the other, it involved sudden immersions (though always as an outsider) into the fiercest, most active bazaars of musical politics, competition, and publicity.

From 1909 to 1914 Sibelius visited Berlin five times (this was initially the aesthetic sphere with which he was most concerned) and Paris and London twice each. Each visit to the German and French capitals – and each intersection with the new continental ideas then circulating in England – precipitated a wave of self-doubt and occasioned a series of painful reflections about his own receding place, or prestige-rating, in the institution of art music, upon which he then brooded during the longer periods of solitude at Ainola. His successful trip to the United States in May and June 1914, for which he composed *The Oceanides*, represents a pre-war capping of his newly consolidated compositional *persona*, now about to embark on the Fifth Symphony, which, as we shall see, would exemplify a reconsidered set of compositional principles.

When did Sibelius begin to feel eclipsed as a modernist? Certainly not, it would seem, before 1909. His much-discussed turn away from an overtly lyrical 'national romanticism' toward a leaner, condensed 'classicism' during the years 1905–09 (its full arrival came with the Third Symphony in 1907) was hardly a rejection of modernism. On the contrary, perhaps responding to certain 'modern-symphonic' controversies that were prevalent in Germany in the early 1900s,[1] Sibelius was probably trying to redefine what a 'symphony' might be, considered in all the severity and high seriousness of its traditions, under the new, institutional conditions of modernism. This 'modern classicism' was to be an unflinching shoring-up of the seemingly enervated formal principle; a refusal to yield to diffuse sentiment or merely colouristic or picturesque detail; a course-correction or a redressing of the balances; a stern recapturing of the 'lost' symphonic principle on new terms for a new century.[2] More pointedly put, Sibelius's 'modern-classical' aim seems to have been to clench his teeth and forge a more compact, harder-edged music than that of the two leading modernists, Strauss and (especially) Mahler. To be sure, this was risky in an age that was nurturing expansionist, experimental, or proto-expressionist currents (and that had come to know Sibelius through his earlier, more popular or overtly nationalistic works). And by 1909 it was a risk that seemed in danger of not succeeding in the continental marketplace. Nonetheless, these were the terms on which he had chosen to compete.

For the most part during his February–May 1909 trip to London, Paris, and Berlin Sibelius's dismissals of certain aspects of Debussy and several other modernists still ring with the voice of confidence. Having met Debussy in London on 27 February, following a Queen's Hall concert that included the *Prélude à 'L'après-midi d'un faune'* and the *Nocturnes*, Sibelius confided on 1 March to his wife, Aino, 'Yesterday I listened to – and met – Debussy. His compositions are interesting, but – I think he's still just beginning – he trusts in all kinds of trivialities' (III, 143; cf. *II, 107–8).[3] Such a reaction might be expected from the intensely 'serious' Sibelius, then composing the quartet, *Voces intimae*, and on 3 March, we find him revelling both in his own current idiosyncrasies and in the swirl of the modern marketplace: 'I have altogether new points of view in my music. You'll see. It's as if I've been dormant.'

Similarly, on 24 March: 'I find it difficult these days to be "modest" and "humble".' At the close of his English visit, on 27 March, having now met with Debussy, D'Indy, and several British composers, and having heard several songs of Debussy, as well as Elgar's First Symphony and Bantock's *Omar Khayyám*, he wrote to his close friend, Axel Carpelan, 'I have seen and heard much [here]. It has also done me a great deal of good – many things that weren't clear to me before are so now. . . . [My musical experiences in England] have all confirmed my thoughts about the path I have taken, take and have to take.' (III, 145, 154, 146; *II, 108, 113, 108–9)

Up to this point Sibelius's intention to continue his modern classicism seems secure enough (although it is not difficult to perceive an underlying *Angst* here). The uncompromisingly spare and 'difficult' *Voces intimae*, sent off to the publisher on 15 April, provided additional confirmation of this and set the seal on his adopted severity. But in Berlin in April and May (where, fearing throat cancer, he was also consulting his medical specialist – and where, we may assume, he continued to immerse himself in the musically new, even as he was completing the terms of his five-year contract with the Berlin publisher Lienau through the quartet and the Op. 57 songs) we sense a growing discontent. From his diary on 21 May 1909: 'Now I must go home. I can't work here any longer. A change of style?' (III, 158; *II, 116)

Sibelius may have questioned his classical turn during this visit to Berlin, but he reaffirmed it only a month later, back at Ainola, in a letter to Carpelan on 20 July 1909:

[1] When I think of these Kapellmeisters with their circus showmanship (they only want pieces to highlight their particular tricks) along with those idiots, the critics, tearing apart this new work, I am lost in admiration of your profound understanding and your solid artistic judgements. [2] You mention interconnections between motives and other such matters that I have done subconsciously. [Only] afterwards can one discern this or that [relationship], but, for all that, from a broader perspective a composer is merely a vessel. What's essential is this wonderful logic (let us call it God) that governs a work of art. [3] From time to time I get bad reviews with devilish thorns in them, from all of which I can see that the road is leading 'ad astra'. [4] If only I could live. Right now I am so certain of my art. (III, 175; *II, 129–30)

This letter touches on the four major themes that would govern Sibelius's compositional life in the immediately ensuing years: 1) a sober 'classicistic' critique of the modernists against whom he was competing (here especially Mahler and Strauss, but also, by implication, other Austro-Germanic symphonists) and whom he also believed to be embracing the merely sensational, the theatrical, or the undisciplined expansive, thus neglecting formal concentration or the seriousness of art itself (in the ensuing years, this criticism would tilt away from the modernists and toward the composers of the New Music);[4] 2) an acknowledgment of the importance of the inner logic of his own best music, which he always (disingenuously?) insisted was not rationally plotted during the composition process but arose naturally, or even mystically, apart from his own volition; 3) anxiety, often veering into indulgent self-pity, over the galling lack of acceptance of his modern-classical works in the continental marketplace of 'progressive' compositions (a variant of this theme concerns his inability to escape the 'nationalist' label originally affixed to the earlier, more successful works); 4) a resolute declaration to continue pursuing his increasingly unique musical path.

As Sibelius poured his energies into the Fourth Symphony in 1910 and 1911, Germanic reactions to his more recent works continued to be uncomfortably mixed. Most ominously, the Third Symphony failed to impress its Berlin audience in February 1910, although the relative success of the various premieres of *Voces intimae* in differing cities of 1910 and 1911 must have been heartening. (It was still received as a decisively 'modern' work, as, for example, in Leipzig in early January 1911.)[5] But in a diary entry of 13 May 1910, one senses that the pressure of the continentally 'new' was now beginning to grow: 'Don't let all these "novelties", triads without thirds and so on, take you away from your work. Not everyone can be an innovating genius. As a personality and "eine Erscheinung aus den Wäldern" [an apparition from the woods] you will have your small, modest place.' (III, 191; *II, 139–40)[6]

Still working on the Fourth Symphony, Sibelius revisited Berlin (following an appearance in Christiania (Oslo)) for about three weeks beginning in mid-October 1910. This seems to have been a crucial trip, during which he intersected with even more emphatic examples of 'New Music', all of which, considered along with the notable failure of a performance of his Violin Concerto, suggested that his own high-risk 'modern-classical' project might no longer be in step with the times. Thus begins in earnest his passage from the first to the second phase of modernism – a passage that would be made all the more painful by his position as an outsider. His harshest critique – in which the term 'modern' now takes on a different connotation – was written to Rosa Newmarch on 1 January 1911. Knowing, of course, that she would share his views, he reported that in Berlin 'as usual I acquired an unconquerable distaste for the "modern tendency". And out of this grew a sense of solitude [*Alleingefühl*]. . . . To my astonishment I see that my works are being performed a good deal on the continent, although they have no "Modernity" in them.'[7] What had Sibelius experienced there? The details are currently unclear. We know, though, that Busoni had introduced him to the young Edgard Varèse (*II, 147), and it may also have been during this trip that Busoni began to discuss Schoenberg's music and ideas with Sibelius.[8]

Back in Finland Sibelius's insecurities began to mount. Reacting to more bad reviews from the continent, he wrote into his diary on 3 November 1910, 'Am I really only a "nationalistic" curiosity? The type who should yield the path to any [more international] vagabond whatever?' (III, 216; *II, 160) Most significantly, on 4 December 1910, four days before his birthday, he entered the following self-assessment:

I have these 44 years of mine. Soon 45. A 'recognized name'. Well, yes, that's all. And all those lovely dreams! This is the result of my return to 'classicism'! But [your] inner voice? Go your own modest but sure way. Glorious Ego, you won't be any the worse [for that]. (III, 218; *II, 161)

The despair now continues to echo through the diary. On 22 January 1911, anticipating a brief February stopover in Berlin – lasting, at most, three or four days – on the way to Riga as part of a Gothenburg-Riga concert tour (and in response to even more bad reviews): 'Been "down" the last few days. . . . The *Berliner Tageblatt* maintains that my earlier works were good, *but* – and so on – and that now my imagination has deserted me! It's difficult to live this life!' (III, 223; *II, 165)

Understanding this context helps to clarify the aesthetic intent of the Fourth Symphony, which received its premiere in Helsinki on 3 April 1911 (and which seemed to stir controversy – often uncomprehending dismissals – wherever it was performed in the next few years). As Sibelius's modern-classical project began to founder in the volatile continental marketplace, he had been furnishing it with increasingly extreme offerings – first the Violin Concerto and *Pohjola's Daughter*, then the Third Symphony and *Night Ride and Sunrise*, and now, in the period of deepest crisis, *Voces intimae* and the Fourth Symphony. In each composition Sibelius had dug in his heels more deeply, doubtless with the aim of increasing his bid in the modernist sweepstakes from the standpoint of his 'Northern', austere, and idiosyncratic classicism. The initial assessment in Helsinki of the Fourth Symphony that seems to have coincided most with Sibelius's own hopes was that of Otto Andersson in the *Tidning för Musik*, who heard it as a 'synthesis of classicism, romanticism, and modernism' that, although difficult, was still capable of providing a model for 'the music of the future'. (III, 232; *II, 172)

Another aspect of the Fourth Symphony, though, one that was destined to be much repeated in subsequent Sibelius commentaries, was its 'sharp protest against the current compositional fashion' (to quote the review of Evert Katila in the 11 April 1911 *Uusi Suometar*). Carpelan amplified the idea in a Gothenburg newspaper, and his commentary (which doubtless originated with the composer himself) was reprinted in the 26 April 1911 *Helsingin Sanomat*:

As a whole the symphony can be regarded as a protest against the prevalent musical style . . . above all in Germany, the home of the 'symphony', where instrumental music is becoming mere technique, a kind of musical civil-engineering, which tries to disguise its inner emptiness behind an enormous mechanical apparatus. (III, 232; *II, 172)

In a letter to Rosa Newmarch on 2 May 1911 Sibelius rephrased this 'protest' idea and added that the Fourth Symphony 'has nothing, absolutely nothing of the circus about it' (III, 232; *II, 172). One must be cautious here. The protest in question – certainly against what he perceived as the diffuse expansionism of Mahler and the technological sensationalism of Strauss and the younger Straussians – was still delivered from the standpoint of one hoping to contend in the modern arena. (Compare, for example, his use of the term 'circus' in his 20 July 1909 letter to Carpelan, quoted above.) The Fourth's protest was to be primarily a modernist advance, not a retreat, and Sibelius hoped to be uttering it from a position of strength. Still, since it was uttered after his important 1910 trip to Berlin, it also contained a suggestion of a withdrawal from the arena of 'progress'.

All of this participates, of course, in a far more general European musical upheaval. The Fourth Symphony's premiere was flanked by two events more crucial for the fate of symphonic modernism: the premiere in Dresden of Strauss's *Der Rosenkavalier* on 26 January 1911 and the death of Gustav Mahler on 18 May 1911. Nothing is currently known of Sibelius's response to either event, but neither could have gone unnoticed. Considered in retrospect, both ceded the Austro-Germanic sphere of *avant-garde* authority to expressionism and the Schoenbergians. A parallel story could be told of Paris on 13 June 1911, where as part of the Summer Ballets Russes offerings Stravinsky's *Petrushka* would take command of the musically new, decisively overtaking the Debussy style, not to mention that of the more orthodox D'Indy and Dukas. (Ravel's glitteringly hedonistic – and coolly mechanistic – *Daphnis et Chloë* would follow in 1912; Stravinsky's *Le Sacre du printemps* in 1913.)

Needless to say, none of this seemed quite so inevitable in mid-1911, but Sibelius was beginning to sense his own eclipse as a contending modernist. This was confirmed during his trip to Paris for much of November and early

December 1911, preceded by a brief, late-October visit to Berlin. Once again plunging into the musical whirl of the city (and apparently trying, without much enthusiasm, to revive some of his profligacy of his youth), he doubtless heard much talk about this new Stravinsky, actually heard a performance of the latter's *Scherzo fantastique*, and was introduced to M. D. Calvocoressi, then a prominent member of the Ravel circle, but not, it seems, to Ravel himself. The impact of this trip may be judged from Sibelius's little-known letter to Aino from Paris on 10 November 1911. For us, it marks the moment when Sibelius abandoned his dreams of contending further as a 'progressive':

Let's let the world go its own way. If you, my dear love, want things as I do, let's not allow anything to drag us away from the path on which we know we must go. I mean the direction of my art. Let's leave the competition to the others. But let's grasp our art with a tremendous grip.[9]

Late 1911 and early 1912 initiate the dark night of Sibelius's 'modernist/New Music' crisis. His diary entries at this time display a number of themes: self-doubt followed by a redoubling of his will to follow a solitary path; complaints that his works of the past several years have either not succeeded or have been habitually misunderstood; reflections on what his own role in history might or might not be; and so on. It is also from this period that we find Sibelius's earliest documentable references to Schoenberg. From the diary-entry of 8 May 1912: 'Arnold Schoenberg's theories interest me even if I find him one-sided. Perhaps I wouldn't if I were to get to know him better.' But on 5 June: 'You won't be any "greater" by outdoing – or trying to outdo – your contemporaries in terms of a revolutionary "profile". Let's not join in any race.' (III, 290; *II, 218)

The presence of the New Music – especially (but by no means exclusively) the music of Schoenberg – was now a reality in Sibelius's life. On around 24 or 25 September 1912 he arrived in England to participate in the Birmingham Festival with his Fourth Symphony – which was to be paired with the premiere of Elgar's *The Music Makers* – and fell once again into the Granville Bantock-Rosa Newmarch-Ernest Newman circle. And surely one of the first things he learned was that Sir Henry Wood had just given the controversial first performance of Schoenberg's Five Pieces for Orchestra, Op. 16, only three weeks earlier, on 3 September, as part of the Promenade Concert season. (This was, of course, the famous premiere at whose rehearsals Wood exhorted the Queen's Hall Orchestra, 'Stick to it, gentlemen! Stick to it! This is nothing to what you'll have to play in twenty-five years' time!')[10] In short, England was abuzz with reactions to Schoenberg. The confrontation of 'modernism' and the New Music – aesthetic, generational, and sociological – had now explicitly entered the public sphere. Indeed, during Sibelius's visit Ernest Newman, comparing the motivic work and concentration of the two composers, pointedly praised the Fourth Symphony at the expense of Schoenberg (*II, 220). (It might be added that another, later novelty of the festival was Scriabin's *Prometheus*, whose mystical and religious claims impressed Sibelius, although he seems not to have attended this performance.)[11]

After Sibelius's trip to England – and after the much-publicized *Pierrot lunaire* events in Germany and Austria (a 16 October 1912 premiere in Berlin followed by a tour of eleven cities) – the tone in his diaries becomes more withdrawn, sterner. By 7 November 1912 we find him referring to the younger generation of composers as his 'natural enemies' (III, 180; *II, 132) – the epithet would resurface during the early stages of the composition of the Fifth Symphony, on 19 December 1914 (IV, 26). In early 1913, the year of *The Bard* and *Luonnotar*, bad news about the Fourth Symphony from Sweden and elsewhere plunged him into despair once again. 'Now don't lose your nerve – and above all your head,' he wrote into his diary on 20 February. 'They see me – at least, the world's leading musicians – as dead. But *nous verrons*. Is this now the end of the composer Jean Sibelius?' (III, 318; *II, 240)[12]

From 5 January to 13 February 1914, after a year in Finland, Sibelius ventured out of his Finnish isolation to visit Berlin once again and to work on *The Oceanides*, his new 'American' commission. Berlin's musical institutions had now been markedly transformed by the inclusion of the New Music, and Sibelius seems to have attended as many events as possible. The available documents (more completely transcribed in Tawaststjerna's biography) display Sibelius the 'outsider's' confrontation with this new whirl – a curious blend of fascination, admiration, and skepticism. For example:

(26 January, to Carpelan) Whenever I hear new works by colleagues, I become more and more convinced that my music has infinitely more nature and life than these hothouse *Erzeugnisse*.

(28 January, diary) A song of Schoenberg made a deep impression on me.

(4 February, diary) Mahler's Fifth Symphony and Schoenberg's *Kammersymphonie*. I suppose that one can see things in this way. But it does hurt the ears. A result achieved by excessive cerebration. People whistled and shouted. Not for weak minds, the so-called talents. They would really make nonsense [of it]. [There is] something great behind it. But Schoenberg certainly doesn't carry it out.

(9 February, diary) Heard Duparc's songs, Korngold's Trio and Schoenberg's [Second]

Quartet, Op. 10. It gave me a lot to think about. He interests me exceptionally. (III, 343–4; *II, 261–2)

That Sibelius could have been impressed by Schoenberg's motivic integrity, rigorous logic, and musical compression is hardly surprising. By this time, however – holding firm to his own variant of his generation's modern programme – he had committed himself to a different path. This was one that he considered less pretentiously contrived, less artificial; one that sought to uncover a deeply intuitive and nature-mystical relationship to sound itself through a process of meditative inwardness and ruthless self-criticism.[13] Notwithstanding the enthusiasm for his work in the more 'cautious' England and the United States, he now realized that as far as the 'progressive' continent was concerned, as an eclipsed modernist he would have to pursue this path as more an outsider than ever.

Reassessed compositional principles, 1912–15:
the five central concepts

Peaking in 1912 after the discouraging continental reception of his Fourth Symphony, Sibelius's Modernist/New Music crisis encompasses both compositional and sociological issues. The 'emancipation of the dissonance', for instance, was not merely an up-to-date harmonic preference. More fundamentally, it was a high-profile surface component of a growing artistic and culture-critical wave that was challenging the musical institutions of European liberal-bourgeois culture that the earlier modernists (the 'Generation of the 1860s') had been committed to nourishing. With its multiplicity of individualized accents, the triadically based, post-Wagnerian musical language of the 1889–1914 period was far from a culturally neutral system to be approached only in technical terms; rather, it was a sign of the institution of art music with which it was inextricably linked. Put another way, a key feature of symphonic modernism's musical language was that it thematized not only its ostensible 'content' (Till Eulenspiegels, fauns, Tuonelan swans, transfigurations and resurrections, seascapes, landscapes, and so on) but also the sociopolitical currents in which it thrived. When composers continued to reflect on (and with) that language in imperiled times, they were simultaneously affirming the continued validity of the cultural principles that had stirred those currents in the first place. This generational or cultural clash lay at the heart of the Modernist/New Music crisis that was spreading throughout prewar Europe.

Thus it is short-sighted to reduce the issue to an aesthetically 'correct' choice of a harmonic language with a quantifiable dissonance quotient. The delivery system apparatus of the modern orchestra, the institution of the public concert, the highly developed, often monumental musical genres themselves with their elevated or serious themes and their grand manner of posing and resolving problems – all of these things, too, were socially and generationally coded, and by the second decade of the twentieth century the codes had grown irksome to the leading edge of younger radicals. The principal orchestral genres associated with the preceding period of modernism – symphony, symphonic poem, and virtuoso concerto (not to mention monumental cantata, orchestral song cycle, or post-Wagnerian opera) – seemed now to be collapsing in favour of such things as the Schoenbergian *Stück* and the Stravinskian ballet-tableau.

Sibelius's *The Bard* (1913, rev. 1914), *Luonnotar* (1913), *The Oceanides* (1914), and the Fifth Symphony (1914–19) were the initial members of a series of works of private brooding, concerned, among other things, with the mortality of their own obsolescing genres and musical language and with the near-insolubility of the problems that they set out to address. These problems involved the bringing into tension of two opposed concepts, both of which were fundamental to his musical thinking. On the one hand were his obsessions with such static things as harmonic near-immobility and the slowly transforming sound-sheet (for example, *The Swan of Tuonela* or the principal thematic area of *Pohjola's Daughter*); elemental, circular repetition (the second themes of the finale of the Second Symphony and the Violin Concerto, the finale of the Third Symphony); ostinatos and pedals; and, especially after 1905, certain classicizing architectural effects (structures unfolded 'as if in quotation marks'), such as the terse, neo-schematic sonata-form of the Third Symphony's first movement. On the other hand were such linear-progressive concerns as: his drive to produce an evolutionary motivic process that ultimately arrives – often triumphantly – at an unmistakable goal or resolution; his growing suspicion of the redundancy of non-altered, or even modestly altered, reprises; and his regard for modern demands for constant originality. Although these issues had occupied Sibelius before (they were primary concerns of all the moderns), in the post-Fourth Symphony period they became crises. They were aggravated further by his decision to reject the 'emancipation of the dissonance' and the emerging world-view of the New Music culture in order to explore further the institution of the symphony and its increasingly suspect, and certainly endangered, triadic language.

In this context of deteriorating norms both Sibelius's past career and his present instincts suggested that the only possible resolution of these problems lay in a compensatory rethinking of symphonic form. In other words, the historic-aesthetic weakness of retaining a triadically based grounding in tonality was to be counterbalanced by an extraordinarily heightened formal concentration. Symphonic form was now to be brought back to its first principles. It was to be reconstituted from the ground floor up. Consequently, after the Fourth Symphony (which, for all of its remarkable textural and harmonic idiosyncrasies, does not emphatically pose the problem of form itself) Sibelius concentrated on the problem of recreating 'form' on a more elemental level. This meant striving to create *ad hoc* musical structures that would be supported less by the horizon of expectations provided by the *Formenlehre* tradition than by the idiosyncratic, quasi-intuitive inner logic of the selected musical materials. Each major composition after the Fourth Symphony represents a relatively unmoored structural experiment that seeks its own course in uncharted formal waters.

The main lines of Sibelius's thought during the post-Fourth Symphony period may be summarized in five central concepts. Each has its roots both in his earlier work and in the work of several of his predecessors and contemporaries. Strictly considered, none is new or unique to this period. The point, though, is that Sibelius now heightens these concepts. And, working together, they come to dominate his musical thinking.

Content-based forms ('fantasias')

Sibelius began to describe this 'radical' intention repeatedly in his diary entries from Spring 1912, exactly the period in which he was anxiously assessing Schoenberg's theories. For example:

(22 April 1912) Musical themes are the things that will determine my destiny.

(23 April 1912) The musical thoughts – the motives, that is – are the things that must create the form and stabilize my path.[1]

(8 May 1912) I intend to let the musical thoughts and their development determine their own form in my soul. (IV, 54; cf. *II, 218)[2]

(1 August 1912) I should like to compare the symphony to a river. It is born from various rivulets that seek each other and in this way the river proceeds wide and powerful toward the sea. But today one excavates the wide, powerful riverbed – that is, one constructs a river. But from where do we get the water? In other words, we don't let the motives and the ideas decide their own form. And despite this we decide to make the river wide and powerful, and we also try to fill it. But, musicians, from where do we get the water? You, dear Ego, noticed this at once.[3]

These remarks signal a wish to tilt further away from a compositional practice in which either the standard *Formenlehre* types themselves (the preformed 'riverbed' of sonatas, song-forms, rondos, and themes and variations) or their late-century deformations are granted a priority in shaping the music's large-scale unfolding. This new, deepened 'modern classicism' was to strive to produce unique structures – freely logical, intuitive, or *ad hoc* shapes – dictated by Sibelius's listening to what might be called the 'will of the selected material'. When passing references to either the standard or the deformational types did occur, they would be a secondary, not a primary, consideration.

Sibelius seems to have identified such aims with the concept of 'fantasia'. This was a term that he was tempted to employ more than once in subsequent years to escape the reification suggested by the more traditional term 'symphony' (see chapter 4 below). In considering the symphony/fantasia dichotomy with which Sibelius would come to struggle, we should notice that his concerns resonate strikingly with A. B. Marx's extended, mid-nineteenth-century description of 'die Fantasie' as the ultimate end-point in the historical evolution of the more schematic forms. 'Only with it is the entire *Formenlehre* brought to its goal, [and] in it, with it, and through it we become free. . . . [Its essence is] the renunciation of all [previously] determined form', and it is a genre not for dabblers, but only for the highest masters, who already 'know all the directions and paths': on virtually a line-by-line basis, Marx's widely known discussion could serve as a grand *apologia* for the deepest aims of Sibelius's post-Fourth Symphony works.[4]

However we might ground Sibelius's thinking historically, it is clear that problems of this sort come increasingly to dominate his works from *The Bard* and *Luonnotar* to his last major composition, *Tapiola* (1926). Later, in retirement, he seems to have regarded the content-based forms of these pieces as his primary contribution to symphonic thinking, and when questioned on his compositional principles, he invariably stressed the intuitive, inspirational, nature-mystical, or non-rational sides of the process. Nearly fifteen years after the composer's death his secretary, Santeri Levas, would recall, 'Sibelius always said that he composed instinctively, never deliberately. . . . For Sibelius music that was written according to formula was not a work of art.' Levas then proceeded to cite a remark of Sibelius (made during the period of retirement, in the 1940s or 1950s):

Thousands of such [formulaic] works have been written . . . and they have all been forgotten. It is often thought that the essence of [a] symphony lies in its form, but this is certainly not the case. The content is always the primary factor, while form is secondary, the music itself determining its outer form. If sonata form has anything that is lasting it must come from within. When I consider how musical forms are established I frequently think about the ice-ferns which, according to eternal laws, the frost makes into the most beautiful patterns.[5]

Such remarks suggest appropriate modes of analysis, at least for the post-1912 works. Here we are to attend *primarily* to the way in which the volitional sound-objects, germinating at the local level, grow 'naturally' and with relatively few preconditions to produce larger architectural shapes. But above all, in coming to understand these larger shapes, we should be prepared to find unusual features for which even such a concept as 'sonata deformation' (or 'free sonata') seems inadequate. It is not that all references to the traditional *Formenlehre* types or their deformations are to be suppressed, but rather that in grappling with the formal processes of Sibelius's unique structures our first appeal need not be to the forms at hand in the textbooks.

Nevertheless, Sibelius also realized that if a new symphonic poem or symphony was to be perceived as a recognizable continuation of its genre, it was still to be in dialogue with some key features of its generic traditions: seriousness of tone; grand sonority, architecture, and rhetoric; thematic and tonal contrasts; some sense of reprise or resolution; and the like. In short, one of Sibelius's most pressing problems had become to create strikingly new, content-based structures that simultaneously touched on a sufficient number of the existing generic conventions to provide an appropriate sense of the social 'occasion' or probable context for its future performances. Within the parameters of the modernist project to which he still clung, he was aggressively ratcheting the *Formenlehre* deformational principle several notches further ahead but by no means abandoning it altogether.

What was needed, then, was a new, more elemental compositional principle that overrode such things as the standard sonata deformations but that also, on a secondary level, permitted the resultant structures to carry on an *ad hoc*, quasi-referential dialogue with selected aspects of the more traditional structures. To judge from the resulting compositions, Sibelius appears to have found this principle in large-scale, circular restatements of multithematic blocks.

Rotational form (varied multisectional strophes)

As mentioned above, one of the features of the earlier Sibelius style had been the insistent repetition of a short melodic phrase or set of phrases: a momentary withdrawal from linear time in favour of 'circular' stasis. In early Sibelius its grimly determined, repetitive effect often asks to be perceived as an identifier of a Finnish folk ethos, that is, as a 'primitive' renunciation of elaborated periodic or florid structure to embrace the incantatory reiterations of an epic or mythic formulaic phrase. The 1898 song, 'Illalle', Op. 17 No. 6, for example, consists entirely of fourteen statements, some varied, of an eleven-note recitation figure. Even when the characteristic melodic intonations and metric configurations of Kalevalaic recitation are lacking, as they are here, the principle of open-ended, potentially infinite restatements of a reciting-phrase is unmistakable. Such procedures helped to establish Sibelius's early reputation as an exotic composer.

It was doubtless also from Russian symphonic composition, which at least from Glinka's *Kamarinskaya* onward had also explored circular stasis, that Sibelius learned of some of the most common generic slots within a 'nationalistic' symphony or concerto for such repetitive 'peasant' themes. These included the scherzo's trio and especially the first or (even more characteristically) the second theme of the finale – as a kind of 'concluding' device or reductive 'folk-goal' of the entire work: one thinks, for example, of Tchaikovsky's Second and Fourth Symphonies or the Violin Concerto; and even Stravinsky's early Symphony in E♭ and, for that matter, the conclusion of *The Firebird* pay homage to the convention. In Sibelius the Second Symphony (three reiterations of the second theme in the finale's exposition, eight in its recapitulation) and the Violin Concerto have already been mentioned in this respect, and to them we might add the earlier *En Saga* and *Lemminkäinen's Return*. (The Fourth Symphony is also exemplary, but less obvious.) More remarkably, the entire finale of the Third Symphony is overtaken by the reiterative principle. And when the Fifth Symphony drives ultimately to the circular 'Swan Hymn' of its finale, it is this convention that provides its most immediate ancestry.

Of course, we need not derive the principle of circularity exclusively from Russian sources. Within the Austro-Germanic tradition one may recall the circular patterns found, say, in much of Schubert or in certain characteristic passages of Bruckner, a composer with whom Sibelius was profoundly impressed. Whatever its composite sources might have been, in forging his own individually accented modern style, Sibelius clearly encouraged the reiterative principle – with its connotations of unflinching inevitability, temporal stasis, and the flight from a linear into a mythic sense of time – to invade increasingly significant portions of his compositions at both local and broader levels.

Of particular interest are instances when Sibelius encourages the rotational principle to take over an entire extended section or movement. The second movement of the Third Symphony, swaying repetitively through its phrase-successions, seems paradigmatic here (along with its rotational finale), as does each half of the important symphonic poem *Night Ride and Sunrise* (1909), which foreshadows so much that is to come in the later works. Its second portion, the 'Sunrise', is especially clear in this respect. Here, after the *Largamente* transition passage (beginning at rehearsal No. 37), we encounter an initial succession of three differing melodic blocks: at Nos. 40 (the 6/4 theme in the woodwinds), 41 (the broad 3/2 'sunrise' idea in the horns, then transferred to the strings), and 44 (the oboe postlude phrase, repeated an octave higher in the flute). The three-melody pattern is then recycled, and slightly expanded, in a more fully realized orchestral texture. Thus we are presented with two broad rotations of a thematically composite, larger block. Clearly, this cyclical procedure, which seems to stand transfixed ('mystically', Sibelius would probably insist) as it attends ever more deeply to the 'inevitable' sound-events rotating past, is most closely related to the *Formenlehre* category of strophic variation. (In some instances it is for all practical purposes identical with it.)

Sibelius would develop this procedure further in his post-1912 works. Strictly considered, a rotational structure is more of a process than an architectural formula. In such a process Sibelius initially presents a relatively straightforward 'referential statement' of contrasting ideas. This is a series of differentiated figures, motives, themes, and so on (which themselves, of course, unfold according to the principle of content-based forms, although they may also be arranged to suggest such things, for example, as a sonata exposition). The referential statement may either cadence or recycle back through a transition to a second broad rotation. Second (and any subsequent) rotations normally rework all or most of the referential statement's material, which is now elastically treated. Portions may be omitted, merely alluded to, compressed, or, contrarily, expanded or even 'stopped' and reworked 'developmentally'. New material may also be added or generated. Each subsequent rotation may be heard as an intensified, meditative reflection on the material of the referential statement.

We shall forgo a discussion here of *The Bard*, whose structural processes, although both rotational and teleological (see p. 26 below), are also extraordinarily subtle and difficult to use as an introductory illustration. But we might pause on its successor, *Luonnotar*, also from 1913. A powerful setting of selections of the *Kalevala* creation story, *Luonnotar* unfolds entirely as a broad double rotation. Its referential statement provides a bar-like sequence of events: introduction – *A* / expanded introduction – expanded *A'* / *B*. Within this referential statement one finds a subrotational pattern in which the first unit (introduction – *A*), in F♯ minor (dorian-inflected), is immediately recycled and expanded to form a second unit (whose *A'* begins with 'Laskeusi lainehille'). Moreover, within each of the two complementary units we find smaller ostinatos and other reiterative material – cycles within cycles. For the *B*-block ('Voi, poloinen, päiviäni!') Sibelius shifts to a contrasting pitch centre, a static 'B♭ minor' chord (blurrily juxtaposing $\frac{5}{3}$ and $\frac{6}{3}$ above the B♭ bass). Once stated in its entirety, the referential statement then cycles freely (in response to the text) through a second, broader rotation. This consists of another, larger, $AA'B$ ('Tuli sotka, suora lintu' / 'Teenkö tuulehen tupani' / 'Niin silloin ve'en emonen'), in which A remains on F♯, A' shifts up onto 'B♭ minor', and B drifts down through G♯ back to the F♯ tonic and ends in the major. The bithematic referential statement, the developmental quality of much of the second rotation, and the F♯ resolution of the B-block at the end also suggest, albeit remotely, aspects of a sonata deformation, although the rotational principle clearly has the upper hand. (I should also add that while the *Formenlehre* term 'strophic variation' is not irrelevant here, its use in this instance would imply an underlying stanzaic background presence in the poetry that does not exist. This is one reason why I prefer the more neutral term 'rotational form'.)

Teleological genesis ('phenomenological' reflection)

As an individual composition's processes unfold, the mature Sibelius often uses them as a matrix within which something else is engendered, usually a decisive climax or final goal (*telos*). The concept of a composition as gradually generative towards the revelation of a higher or fuller condition is character- istic of the modern composers. Strauss's *Death and transfiguration* and *Also sprach Zarathustra* are paradigmatic here,[6] as are the finales of many of Mahler's symphonies. (On a broader level, of course, it is also the driving principle of all resolving structures.) A useful example from the pre-1912 Sibelius is the slow movement of the Fourth Symphony, which gradually generates a *telos* theme out of disparate fragments. As we shall see, the Fifth Symphony is ordered on many structural levels by the principle of teleological genesis.

When combined with a rotational structure that progressively becomes more complex or 'revelatory' with each cycling, teleological genesis can take on an elemental, mythic effect: the patient rocking of the cradle, or the ritualistic nurturing or preparing for the birth of something new. At the very core of the Fifth Symphony (see chapter 5), this procedure is among the most central features of the post-1912 Sibelius's major compositions. For the Sibelius analyst, it often provides the master key that unlocks the whole. In its classic pattern a mere motivic gesture or hint is planted unobtrusively in an early rotation; it then grows in later rotations and is ultimately fully unfurled – as the *telos* – in the final one. The earliest movement in Sibelius's symphonies to feature this is the scherzo-finale combination of the Third. And combined with such a text of gestation as *Luonnotar* the technique is particularly apt and elementally powerful. Here the *telos* idea, associated with the physical actuality of the world's birth – both its mystery and its pain – is represented in three increasingly potent appearances (Promise / Near Approach / Culmination) of a musical idea that is embedded in but emerges separately out of the 'maternal' rotations. It appears first in the clarinet and bass clarinet below tremolo strings at the end of the referential statement (first rotation). It next appears, more developed into a *forte* triple statement, *rinforzando*, just before the *A'* text of the second rotation, 'Teenkö tuulehen tupani'. Its *telos* version proper, the piece's sonorous climax, marks the passage from the second rotation's *A'*- to its *B*-block, which then proceeds to 'explain' the preceding musical *telos* by providing the textual details of the mythic parturition.

The feminine-gendered aspects of all of this are self-evident: the *Luonnotar* constellation of images brings together literal pregnancy and metaphorical birth,[7] a feminized 'Nature' (its virtually invariable gendering), musically circular or rotational gestations, and, perhaps, the 'feminine' medium of music itself for the telling of this narrative. To be sure, from the point of view of a gender-oriented or feminist musicology there is much to reflect on here. From a different perspective, though, such a procedure – a centripetal drive toward ontological essences that are by no means to be equated with an interest in mere programmatic representation, metaphor, or allegory – also finds a remarkable parallel in the concurrent phenomenology of Husserl and especially, later, that of Heidegger, particularly as found, for example, in the latter's celebrated essay from 1935–6, *Der Ursprung des Kunstwerkes* ('The origin of the work of art'). Heidegger's reflection on the possibility of a deep-sinking into the sheer materiality of things in quest of what, characteristically, he describes as a summoning of '*aletheia*, the unconcealedness of beings' or 'a bringing forth of beings . . . *out of* concealedness and specifically *into* the unconcealedness of their appearance'[8] might remind us both of Bie's 'materialistic' definition of musical modernism in 1906 (see chapter 1 above) and, most obviously, of the sheer power of Sibelius's strained concentration in the major works to call forth certain kinds of primeval or elemental *teloi*. However provocative, such parallels should not be considered absolute: in Sibelius the urge to uncover phenomenological essences is also shot through with a lingering, pan-Romantic nature-mysticism of a distinctly 'generation-of-the-1860s' cast.

Klang meditation

Another guiding force at work in Sibelius throughout his entire career is a heightened attention to *Klang*, the palpability of the sound-object itself (including timbre, chord-spacing, and so on), as a primary expressive and structural element. This is hardly a feature unique to Sibelius,[9] but when coupled with the high focus associated with content-based forms (in which the physical presence or instantaneousness of its timbre is taken as a defining constituent of the volitional sound-object), ever-deepening rotations or meditations, and teleological genesis, *Klang* emerges as an especially prominent musical factor.

Sibelius took pride in the individualized quality of his orchestrations, and he seems to have regarded them with mystical attributes that he associated with the objects, colours, and sounds of nature. Reminded, for example, of the 'low, reddish granite rocks' jutting out of the 'pale blue' Baltic Sea some distance off the Finnish coast, 'solitary islands of a hard, archaic beauty, inhabited by hundreds of white seagulls', he told De Törne, 'When we see those granite rocks we know why we are able to treat the orchestra as we do!'[10] Complementing their rotational or *Formenlehre*-deformational structures, Sibelius's works may also be considered to display *Klang* structures (patterns of orchestration) that intersect with the thematic/harmonic designs in unpredictable ways. At times Sibelius's works strike us as proto-minimalist sound sheets, whose actively moving timbre surfaces are undergirded by a more fundamental, deep-current slow motion. *The Swan of Tuonela* is a well-known early example; from the late works *Tapiola* represents the *ne plus ultra*.

Following *The Bard* and *Luonnotar*, Sibelius's next major orchestral work, *The Oceanides* (1914), displays all the techniques we have encountered so far. Most important for our immediate purposes, this symphonic poem may be considered a direct structural predecessor to much that would happen in Sibelius's next major work, the Fifth Symphony. *The Oceanides* is a three-rotation, sound-sheet piece that also displays features of a free sonata deformation.[11] It should be especially underscored that its particular tri-rotational pattern (the 'Oceanides Pattern') is one that would prove of central importance for the Fifth Symphony: 1) referential statement (or expositional rotation); 2) complementary rotation; 3) free, culminatory rotation (releasing the climactic *telos*, whose embryonic motives had been nurtured in the earlier rotations).

In *The Oceanides* the first rotation's thematic (but not tonal) design, while not a sonata exposition in the strict *Formenlehre* sense, is nevertheless in dialogue with the expositional principle. Its first thematic area (with the main theme in a pair of flutes) is a broadly expanded cadence in the tonic, D major, and its contrasting 'second theme' is a set of tonally upward-shifting wave sequences (for the most part carried melodically by the reed-woodwinds and coloured by rich harp glissandos) that ends up back on a D – but now minor, not major – that immediately shifts to a B♭ sonority (rehearsal E) to effect a short retransition. The complementary rotation moves through the same materials but deepens the *Klang* and alters the pitch-levels: the first area now articulates a broad F-major cadence, and, darkening ominously in timbre, the second area's sequences (beginning shortly after K) come to an inconclusive close on E♭ minor (letter N). Since it has aspects of both a development and an expositional repeat, one might consider the complementary rotation as something on the order of a 'developmental counter-exposition', provided we do not allow these terms to obtain formal priority. The culminatory rotation (in dialogue with the developmental space of a sonata deformation) is freer and concentrates mainly on the second-theme ideas. In one of the most remarkable *Klang* shifts in the orchestral repertory the second rotation's queasy, timbre-darkening features are now intensified to represent a fully unleashed sea-storm that winds up enormous tension, ultimately to release it in a single blow – the powerful cadential culmination in D major (*Tempo I*, two bars before **R**), the piece's *telos*. Instead of introducing a potentially redundant recapitulation, however – always a problem area for modern composers – this cadence marks the onset of a brief aftermath-coda, a sudden dissipation of the dark storm colours and a prolongation of the D-major tonic.

Interrelation and fusion of movements

This important Sibelian procedure has been widely noted, and we need touch on it only briefly here. From about the time of Liszt's 'Dante' Sonata, B minor Sonata, and orchestral tone poems, and increasingly around the turn of the century, one of the chief issues in symphonic composition had been to create a 'multimovement form in a single movement'. This was a matter of particular importance to Strauss, Sibelius, and Schoenberg.[12] In Sibelius one of the clearest examples occurs in the Third Symphony, in which the third and fourth movements are fused into a rotational scherzo and finale combination, with the finale also serving as a replacement 'recapitulation'. As we shall see, the 1916 and 1919 versions of the Fifth Symphony will fuse an attenuated first movement with a subsequent scherzo (now functioning in part as a recapitulation of a sonata deformation of the breakthrough type, although the whole is more dominated by content-based and rotational-teleological considerations). And all of this will lead to Sibelius's Seventh Symphony, his most extensive exploration of the multimovement form in a single movement.

Related to the multimovement principle was the direct 'organic' interrelation of movements through the sharing of motives or even larger blocks of material. Although the basic notion has deep roots in standard symphonic practice, some of the modernists explored it in unorthodox ways. Numerous instances are to be found in Mahler, who, to cite merely one example, based portions of his Fifth Symphony's second movement on some of the material of the first. Similarly (and perhaps partially in response to the Mahler work, which we know he studied carefully),[13] the second movement of Sibelius's quartet, *Voces intimae*, recomposes material from its first. A somewhat different procedure may be found in Sibelius's Fourth Symphony. Here the four movements subdivide into two two-movement pairs. In both pairs the second movement springs to life out of the final sonority of its predecessor; the content of the latter emerges out of the implications of the former. Moreover, one of the functions of the third movement's teleological genesis is explicitly to plant (in the clarinets and bassoons fourteen bars from its end) the thematic seed that will shoot forth as the main idea of the finale. The Fifth Symphony would also be deeply concerned with such interrelational principles.

4

Of Heaven's door and migrating swans: composing a confession of faith

In June 1914 Sibelius returned from a month-long visit to the United States. This had been one of the most successful trips of his life. In addition to the various honours bestowed on him by fervent American supporters, the trip had featured his new tone poem, *The Oceanides*, his largest post-Fourth Symphony work to date. Although he returned home in an expansive frame of mind, the sudden onset of the world war at the end of July changed utterly the conditions of his life. Above all, the 'business' aspect of his career fell instantly into tatters. His habitual trips to the principal centres of European music were now unthinkable, and even the hope of publishing significant works outside of Finland became snarled in politics and, in effect, ground to a halt. Thus at the moment when Sibelius was crystallizing a new set of compositional principles, a four-year period of professional stasis was imposed on him. The effect was as if he had been literally banished to the periphery: an eccentric, troubled, broodingly 'mystical' figure residing in emphatically non-'modern' conditions with his family and servants and meditating deeply on the changing seasonal moods and deep silences of Järvenpää's forests, overlooking Lake Tuusula. While, far away (or so it seemed), the European world was changing forever.

In addition to the unavoidably political cast given to all things during the Fifth-Symphony years (1914–19), Sibelius's own personal circumstances loomed large at this time. For the sake of household economy he was continually forced to compose commercially viable trifles – piano pieces, small chamber works, and so on – which he could market to local publishers (such as Westerlund and Lindgren), who had no economic incentive to ask for more complex works. The composition of the grand-scale Fifth Symphony was surrounded on all sides by the rapid manufacturing of musical trinkets conceived on a different plane altogether. In a period of self-redefinition and artistic crisis these things, too, took their toll. Such considerations help to explain the long gestation of the Fifth. From the composer's point of view there was simply no hurry to publish it.

Initial thematic sketches: August 1914 to June 1915

Sibelius had first mentioned the possibility of a Fifth Symphony in a diary entry from 2 March 1912, about eleven months after the premiere of the Fourth: 'Symphony V. Symphony VI. "Luonnotar"! It remains to be seen whether these plans can work out.' (III, 287; *II, 216) The actual starting point for the symphony, however, seems to be datable almost precisely to the beginning of the world war, 29 July 1914. Tawaststjerna reports that Sibelius recorded having conceived a 'beautiful theme' at this time (IV, 5). By 1 August he wrote into the diary, 'The new symphony is beginning to gather speed'; by 2 August, 'I'm forging something new. A symphony? Time will tell' (IV, 7); and so on.

From August 1914 until June 1915 the composer was preoccupied with creating and ordering the thematic kernels of this newly projected four-movement symphony (although by December 1914 he would be simultaneously thinking about a Sixth as well). The principal musical document from this period is a forty-page sketchbook (now preserved in the State Archives in Helsinki), whose entries seem hastily scribbled on handwritten staves. Its first thirty-seven pages contain an abundance of thematic sketches directly associated with the Fifth; the final three pages of sketches belong to summer 1916. Tawaststjerna, who provides plates of fifteen pages (IV, following p. 176) and discusses them at length, points out that the sketchbook also contains important thematic material for the Sixth Symphony and for the Violin Sonatina, Op. 80. But in fact one may also find here thematic germs for both the Seventh Symphony and *Tapiola* as well – germs conceived in Fifth-Symphony contexts.

The picture that emerges during this ten- or eleven-month period is that of a composer preoccupied with brief, concentrated ideas, 'nature-mystical' seeds that were suitable for generating the content-based form of larger pieces. As it turned out, the sheer number of undeveloped ideas produced at this time exceeded that appropriate for a single piece. Sibelius's diary remarks from 10 April 1915 are telling:

[It's] warm outside, and the winter is receding. Once again there is a fragrance in the air of the thaw, of youth, and of crime. . . . In the evening [I worked] on the symphony. Arrangement of the themes. This important task, which fascinates me in a mysterious way. It's as if God the Father had thrown down the tiles of a mosaic from heaven's floor and asked me to determine what kind of picture it was. Maybe [this is] a good definition of 'composing'. Maybe not. How would I know! (IV, 55, 102; cf. *I, 244–5)

By the spring of 1915 Sibelius's essential problem had become to sort out the

Example 1

themes and, ultimately, to permit them to refract and develop into the four major works of the next twelve years: the Fifth, Sixth, and Seventh Symphonies, and the tone poem *Tapiola*, all of which, consequently, may be heard as sharing a deep kinship. Or, to adapt the composer's metaphor, each represents a separate sector of the same, quadripartite heavenly mosaic.

In addition to the 1914–15 sketchbook (and possibly a few scattered, related sketch pages), we should mention Sibelius's letter to his confidant, Axel Carpelan, from 22 September 1914 – at the earliest stages of this process of thematic discovery: 'Once again in a deep valley. But I'm already beginning to see dimly the mountain I shall surely climb. . . . For an instant God opens his door and *His* orchestra plays the Fifth Symphony.' (IV, 22 and Pl. 2 after p. 176) Above this last sentence Sibelius wrote the music transcribed in Ex. 1. Two aspects of it are notable: it is more thickly conceived than most of the ideas noted in the sketchbook, and its initial three bars seem unrelated to any of the Fifth Symphony sketchbook themes. It remains a puzzling, isolated fragment.

By mid or late autumn 1914 Sibelius was able to lay out on p. 12 of the sketchbook his first thematic table for the projected 'Sinf V' (Ex. 2α–ζ). We may use it as a springboard to summarize the composer's musical vision during much of this August-to-June conceptual period – for the Fifth planned at this time was markedly different from what it would become. To judge from Sibelius's diary entries, he associated most of the themes with mystical nature experiences at Ainola. Ex. 2α, the leading thematic idea of a first movement that he would never compose, is a variant of his earliest known thematic idea for the Fifth. Tawaststjerna refers to the many forms of this idea as the 'stepwise impulse' and sees in it one of two grounding gestures that interact dialectically to produce the current Fifth. (The other is the 'swinging impulse', Exx. 2δ1 and ζ2.) Although the α theme proper, along with the movement that it was to dominate, was ultimately discarded, Tawaststjerna

33

Example 2. 1914–15 sketchbook, p. 12 (thematic table)

argues that Sibelius reshaped it to become the woodwind countermelody above the 'Swinging Theme' in the finale (first heard at bars 129ff; IV, 52–3).

On the facing p. 13 Sibelius jotted down a fuller variant of this α theme (Ex. 3: the composer may have intended its final three bars to be an alternative reading to the preceding two). This is almost certainly a sketch for the symphony's opening: as a later, separate orchestral sketch shows, the initial 'motto' was conceived for horns, and we may also note the importance of b♭–e♭¹–f¹–b♭¹, bars 3–6, which would play an important role in the opening of the post-1915 versions.[1] The α theme stayed with Sibelius for some time in the sketches, but it ultimately seems to have been 'captured' by a theme that would become the germinal idea for the Sixth Symphony. The first two staves of p. 18 contain an early phase of this capturing (probably from late autumn 1914), although the leading idea here was almost certainly not yet allotted to any projected Sixth Symphony (Ex. 4).

The initially projected second movement (Exx. 2β, γ, and δ) was to become the core of the Fifth Symphony as we know it.[2] A first version (in D minor)

Example 3. 1914–15 sketchbook, p. 13

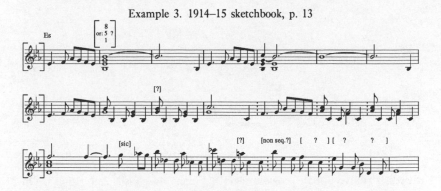

of the eventually discarded β theme had appeared earlier, on p. 8 of the sketchbook, where it was labelled in Swedish as 'Scerzot' ('the scherzo', to which Sibelius later added, 'in Ess', ('in E♭') and wondered whether it should be turned into the second or the third movement). The two γ themes, along with δ2, would eventually provide much of the material for the first two movements of the first, 1915 version, which were subsequently fused to become the complex single movement of the 1916 and 1919 versions. Thus the basic material for the large first movement as we know it today began in scherzo guise: the current first movement grows into the 'natural' form of its material in its second, 'scherzo' portion. We may also note that on this theme table, and also on a variant on the subsequent page (13), Sibelius labelled the δ2 theme 'Aino'. The significance of his wife's name in this context is unclear – her name, in fact, is often found in Sibelius's sketches – but a variant of the theme is one of the chief features of the current scherzo portion of the first movement (beginning with the Allegro moderato, bars 114ff).

In the theme table the crucial 'Swinging Theme', δ1, is assigned both to the scherzo and to the finale (ζ2): clearly, it seems to have been planned as a climactic idea or *telos* of both movements. This, too, was one of Sibelius's first ideas for the symphony, and it is important to notice that in the sketches it invariably appears not in the more normal, 'thematic' shape in which we initially encounter it in the eventual finale (bars 105ff) but rather in the shape in which its intervals are beginning to be splayed open or 'split apart'. In the finale as we know it this feature appears only at the end (bars 435ff). Curiously, a sketch for the 'Swinging Theme' had first appeared on p. 5 of the sketchbook, where, in A♭, it had been joined to a more vigorous idea in the bass (Ex. 5). On a different sketch (p. 11) the vigorous idea appears in 6/8 under the

Example 4. 1914–15 sketchbook, p. 18

Swedish rubric 'Finalen/Bachustståg' ('Finale/Bacchus's Procession'). On both sketchbook pages we may recognize it as an idea that would ultimately find its home in a prolonged 'rustling' passage of *Tapiola*, in which it is shifted to the upper register and written in 12/8 (letter G, bars 208ff): this theme, in fact, is the germinal idea of the future tone poem. (Indeed, since they are all interrelated, as mentioned above, it may be argued that 'Tapiola' – or 'The forest' (literally, 'The place where the god Tapio dwells') – may be regarded as the implied overarching title of Symphonies 5, 6, and 7 as well.)

During the later phases of this initial sketch period, the 'Swinging Theme' – as usual, in this 'split-apart' version – is also found in a provocative diary entry from 21 April 1915 (Ex. 6), which clearly shows that Sibelius strongly identified his music, quasi-pantheistically, with the elemental 'Nature' that he was experiencing at Ainola. The diaries during this particularly active compositional period are also flooded with raptures about the Finnish spring, the melting snow, and the grand migrating birds that so deeply impressed the composer. The relevant entry:

Today at ten to eleven I saw 16 swans. One of my greatest experiences! Lord God, that beauty! They circled over me for a long time. Disappeared into the solar haze like a gleaming, silver ribbon. Their call the same woodwind type as that of cranes, but without tremolo. The swan-call closer to the trumpet, although it's obviously a sarrusophone sound. A low[-pitched] refrain reminiscent of a small child crying. Nature mysticism and life's *Angst*! The Fifth Symphony's finale-theme: [Ex. 6] Legato in the trumpets!! . . . That this should have happened to me, who have so long been the outsider. Have thus been in the sanctuary, today 21 April 1915. (IV, 103)[3]

And a related entry from three days later, 24 April 1915:

The swans are always in my thoughts and give splendour to [my] life. [It's] strange to learn that nothing in the whole world affects me – nothing in art, literature, or music – in the same way as do these swans and cranes and wild geese. Their voices and being.

Example 5. 1914–15 sketchbook, p. 5

[stems added]

Apropos of [my] symphonies. To me they are confessions of faith from the different periods of my life. And from this it follows that my symphonies are all so different.[4] (IV, 103)

Although the 'Swinging Theme' was conceived in late summer or autumn 1914 (over a half-year before these diary entries), it seems either that Sibelius had always associated it with the grace of the swans in flight or that by spring 1915 it came to take on this association permanently. Almost two years later, after the premiere of the symphony's second version, Carpelan wrote to Sibelius on 15 December 1916 in praise of the work, mentioning prominently its finale's 'swan hymn beyond compare' (IV, 195). This is a label that he could have gotten only from the composer; consequently, we shall adopt it from this point onward to identify the theme.[5]

The originally planned theme for the third (slow) movement, one version of which appears in the theme table, Ex. 2ε in B major ('eller Cess', 'or C♭'), is another idea that frequently recurs during this late 1914–early 1915 period. As Tawaststjerna suggests, the theme may be referred to in the diary entry of 10 October 1914: '*Alleingefühl* again. Alone and strong. . . . The autumn

Example 6

Example 7. Thematic sketch for the Seventh Symphony (Kilpeläinen, A/0359)

sun is shining. Nature in its farewell colours. My heart sings sadly – "The shadows lengthen". Fifth Symphony Adagio? That such a poor being as I can have such rich moments!!' (IV, 22) This theme seems to have been one of the Fifth's central features throughout this whole period of initial planning. When Sibelius abandoned the idea, probably in the middle of 1915, it was doubtless with great reluctance. Tawaststjerna does not mention, however, that Sibelius eventually reshaped this grand Adagio-theme into the broadly spanned trombone theme that reappears throughout the Seventh Symphony. An undated subsequent version of this theme among Sibelius's sketches for the Seventh – one of many versions – can help to demonstrate the connection (Ex. 7).[6]

Sibelius's first thoughts for the Fifth's finale, Exx. 2ζ1–3, include an abandoned theme (ζ1), a climactic return of the Swan Hymn (ζ2) that was to have been first sounded in the scherzo, and a third theme (ζ3) stressing the 'Neapolitan' $c\flat^2$–$f\flat^1$. Theme ζ3, of course, eventually found its way into the first movement as its 'second theme', bars 20ff. Here the instructive thing to observe, though, is the motivic relationship between ζ2 and ζ3, which in the familiar version of the symphony are so widely separated. The point is that in the familiar first movement's 'second theme' we may also glimpse the beginnings of a symphony-long shaping toward the melodic *telos* of the whole work, the Swan Hymn. (It should be added that in the 1915 version of the Symphony, the 'Neapolitan' ζ3 idea returns prominently in the finale, where it clearly serves as a reminder of the process that has led to the Swan Hymn. This explicit recall was suppressed in the final version.)

Both the 'Neapolitan' ζ3 theme and the ultimately abandoned ζ1 theme had also appeared on the second staff of an earlier sketch on p. 10 under the rubric 'Intrada (Pastoral ton)'. Curiously, on the first staff of that pastoral 'intrada' sketch one finds a theme that Sibelius would ultimately turn into the slow movement of the Fifth (Ex. 8). Further down on the p. 10 sketch Sibelius also

Example 8. 1914–15 sketchbook, p. 10

toyed with using this theme as the main idea of a song with orchestra that never materialized, 'Goternas Sång' ('Song of the Goths'). Thus the eventual versions of the Fifth represent something of a careful fusion of the theme-table ideas (Ex. 2α–ζ) and what Sibelius thought of later, in 1914, as (possibly) the Sixth Symphony, the pastoral 'Intrada', the aborted 'Goternas Sång' and 'Bacchus's Procession', and perhaps a few other pieces.

Drafts of three – and possibly four – other themes for the eventual Fifth also appear scattered throughout the 1914–15 sketchbook: 1) the finale's *un pochettino largamente* theme, destined to play a central role in that movement's last rotation (bars 407ff; sketchbook, pp. 14, 28, and 29, the last two of these in A minor and D minor, dated 17 and 18 January 1915, but here in the context of Sixth Symphony finale sketches); 2) the scherzo's 'trio theme' (first movement, bars 218ff); 3) a brief but crucially important passage from the eventual slow movement (conceived in the sketchbook as the principal idea of the Sixth Symphony's second movement) that also foreshadows the intervals of what would become a substantial part of the primary theme of the Fifth's finale (Ex. 9;[7] cf. the definitive slow movement, bars 111ff, and see also the discussion of this theme in chapter 5 below); and 4) a theme originally planned for the finale of the Sixth that suggests the head motive of the Fifth's finale (Ex. 10).

The easy interchange of ideas proposed for the Fifth and Sixth Symphonies is one of the prominent features of this creative phase. While Sibelius began creating the themes for the Fifth in August and September 1914, on 2 October he mentions in his diary that he had also 'worked on the new thing' (IV, 22).[8] He mentions this unexplained 'new thing' again on 15 December, and the following day he reports having 'worked on Fantasia I' (IV, 25) – probably identical with the 'new thing'. Tawaststjerna's conjecture that the 'Fantasia' was the Sixth Symphony is doubtless correct, and it is in the January 1915 stages of the sketchbook that the Sixth Symphony's projected themes are first methodically laid out in tables.

In addition to the issues of dating and thematic interchanges between the Fifth and the Sixth, a perhaps even more central problem lies in the

Example 9. 1914–15 sketchbook, p. 23

implications of the title, 'Fantasia'. Already on 18 October Sibelius had confided to his diary, concerning the Fifth, 'I wonder whether this name "symphony" has done more harm than good to my symphonies. I'm really planning to let my inner being – my fantasy – speak.' (IV, 23) Similarly, on 26 November, 'But – as long as they are – then they really are symphonies. One needs to broaden the concept.' But again on 21 December: 'Worked on the orchestral fantasia.' (IV, 26) These entries recall both his 1912 plan to write an 'Erste Phantasie für grosses Orchester Op. 67!!' as well as a 'Zweite, etc.' (5 May 1912; III, 287; *II, 216) and, above all, his new *credo* of 1 August 1912, in which he declared himself prepared to abandon the standard *Formenlehre* structures to permit his ideas to 'decide their own form' (see chapter 3 above).

In Sibelius's late-1914 restating of the issue we can again see the depth of the symphonic problems that he was now facing. Upon undertaking the Fifth, and now beginning to think about a Sixth as well, he was wondering whether his new commitment to content-based forms would produce works that should be received as standing outside the genre of the symphony. In this sense of marking pronounced departures from traditional architectural schemes, Symphonies 5 and 6 could both be heard as fantasias. Still, it was probably because of their eventual, more traditional multimovement scaffolding that Sibelius decided to retain the generic rubric 'symphony'. This sets up a substantially different horizon of expectations for the listener than would 'fantasia'; far from being trivial, few issues could be more fundamental. *Tapiola* may also be regarded as a fantasia (in the sense of an emphatically non-normative, content-driven symphonic structure), and we may recall that the Seventh Symphony was first performed in 1924 under the title, 'Fantasia sinfonica'. (Here again, its multimovement implications were doubtless among the factors that convinced Sibelius to publish it as a symphony.) It is evident that the problem of genre – symphony or fantasia – was one on which Sibelius would brood throughout this period of composition, and, as I have

Example 10. 1914–15 sketchbook, p. 23

proposed in chapter 3 above, it is an important element of his compositional thinking at this time.

The 1915 version

By June 1915 the Fifth Symphony appears to have been little more than two or three scattered tables of potential themes that still needed weeding, developing, and binding together. The impetus to do so came from musical Finland's plans to mark Sibelius's fiftieth birthday, 8 December 1915, with a gala festival in Helsinki lasting several weeks. The festivities were to feature performances of the composer's most recent works, and the new Fifth was to be its centrepiece. The contrast between these celebratory, outward preparations and the tortured entries in Sibelius's diary during the last half of 1915 could not be more stark: as was all too normal, the private entries spill over with fears about monetary debts, reactions to real or imagined slights, feelings of isolation and abandonment, indulgent self-pity and sarcasm, and anguished aesthetic self-reassessments.

'All the threads lead toward the Fifth', he noted on 11 July 1915 (IV, 127), but there is little evidence of his having taken up the work in earnest until September. The cranes reappeared in Järvenpää on the 5th ('I saw the cranes migrating and singing out their music. I again learned [about] the spontaneity of sound' [IV, 135]), and shortly thereafter the symphony was underway again. From a diary entry marked 6–14 September: 'These days I have been living in the symphony, which is now turning out to be grand and resonant.' (IV, 135) But the obvious problem was, 'Can I get the symphony ready in time for 8 December? It looks bleak. *Mais nous verrons.*' (22 September 1915, IV, 135) The same fear arises on 13 October: 'I'm still tracing out the broad [symphonic] lines. But I'm concerned that there won't be time for the details and for the writing of the fair copy. But I have to find time.' (IV, 138)

Sibelius's compositional activity at this time (about which we know virtually nothing) must have been as prodigious as his own personal affairs and daily life were convulsed and chaotic. He now focussed his scattered themes into a four-movement piece whose thematic and expressive substance was, notwithstanding a few deviations, essentially the same as that of the third version of the work that we know today. As a conceptually coherent work, the Fifth Symphony seems to have been put together in three months, from the beginning of September to the end of November 1915. 1 November: 'The first movement of the Fifth Symphony is ready and will be sent off tomorrow.' 2 November: 'Notes at the copyist's.' 8 November: 'Second movement: Allegro commodo at the copyist's.' 11 November: 'I'm working on the second movement' [*sic*: third?]. 15–16 November: 'Third movement ready. Tomorrow to the copyist.' (IV, 139) As Sibelius was completing the symphony's finale, his twenty-one-year-old daughter Katarina noted in her own diary on 30 November: 'Papa stays awake every night until 5 o'clock, then sleeps until 12 or 12:30 – or lies in bed, since he himself stubbornly claims to be working in bed.' (IV, 140)

Following a week of rehearsals, on 8 December 1915, his fiftieth birthday, Sibelius began the celebrations in his honour by conducting the premiere of the first version of the Fifth with the City Orchestra in the auditorium of Helsinki University. Preceding the Fifth on the programme were *The Oceanides* and the Two Serenades for Violin and Orchestra, Op. 69, with Richard Burgin as soloist. Curiously, the programme for this gala premiere provides slightly differing tempo designations for the first two movements from those available on the surviving parts: on the programme, *Tempo tranquillo assai. Quasi attacca al / Allegro co nininciando* [*sic*: read *cominciando*] *moderato e poco a poco stretto*; from the parts, *Tempo moderato assai. / Allegro commodo*.[9] The discrepancy may have arisen from the haste with which the programme was put together, or it may represent an actual state of the movement titles – one that may either predate or postdate the copyist's parts, since there would have been no reason for any of this to have been 'corrected' on each of the parts. (And no imminent printing of the work being planned.)

No copy of the full manuscript score from 1915 is known to exist, but the work may readily be reassembled from its orchestral parts, which survived intact and are now housed at the Helsinki University Library. A still unpublished full score, in fact, was prepared from them for a second performance in 1970, some thirteen years after the composer's death, by the Helsinki City Orchestra under Jorma Panula. A few copies of the audio tape of this performance, never released commercially, have made their way into the hands of various Sibelians over the past years, and its most basic differences from the final version were noted in print by the late 1970s.[10]

By far the fullest description of the 1915 version is to be found in the fourth volume of Tawaststjerna's Sibelius biography. Here, in addition to his general discussion (IV, 142–7), which includes ten music examples, six of them from the original finale, one may also find a separate appendix containing a set of comparative tables that schematically list the broad structural differences among the three versions (IV, 377–86). Because all of this will be available in English before too long, our summary here can be briefer and will cite examples that Tawaststjerna does not provide. For those awaiting the translation of the Finnish volume, however, it should be added that although the discussion below is written from a quite different point of view, it does strive to incorporate the essential information to be found in Tawaststjerna's book.

(A further word of caution might still be in order. Reading capsulized descriptions of 'early versions' can be an annoyingly abstract enterprise, particularly when, as is the case here, we are concerned with preliminary versions for which neither printed scores nor commercial recordings are readily available. My treatment of the two early versions here – 1915 and 1916 – presupposes a close acquaintance with the final, 1919 score, which I describe in some detail in chapter 5. Moreover, since for the sake of both conciseness and precision the discussion below refers to terms and concepts exemplified more fully in chapter 5, some readers might find it helpful to consult that chapter concurrently with what follows in this one.)

As has been mentioned earlier, the central feature of the 1915 version, as opposed to the later ones, is that it consisted of four separate movements, not three. As we shall see, in the following year Sibelius revised and fused together the original first two movements – a moderately paced first movement followed by an *Allegro commodo* scherzo – to produce the large, compound single movement that begins the (largely unknown) 1916 and (very familiar) 1919 versions. The first issue to consider here, therefore, concerns the shape and boundaries of the original first movement.

In 1915 the first movement began with a simpler presentation (Ex. 11) of what we would recognize as the final version's bars 3ff (cf. the 1919 opening, Ex. 15, on p. 61). The 1915 opening stresses the initial 'ii$^6_5$' chord as an important, generative sonority, and it explicitly recalls, of course, the opening of Beethoven's Piano Sonata, Op. 31, No. 3, as well as that of Sibelius's own *Lemminkäinen and the Island Maidens*. This 'ii^7' in various positions (but often suggesting a resonant $^6_4$ over A♭, although other actual chordal pedals in the lowest voice are not uncommon) seems to have had a special significance for Sibelius: we may also find it spotlighted, for example, in *Night Ride and Sunrise*

Example 11. 1915 version, mvmt 1, bars 1–13

(for instance, 1 bar before and 6–7 bars after No. **42**); and the same sonority figures prominently in the Seventh Symphony, 4–6 bars after **T**, where it echoes several similar chords – at differing pitch levels – earlier in the work. In Ex. 11 we should also observe that the original opening of the Fifth featured a static swaying between the 'ii⁰₅' and the neighbouring 'I⁰₅' (note especially the horn accents on the fourth beat of bars 1, 3, and 5) – an important procedure to which we shall return in discussing the 1919 version. In addition, its melodic material differed slightly from that of the final score. The types of variants found in these opening measures (again, see the more familiar Ex. 15) are characteristic of the local melodic differences that the present-day listener would notice in several portions of the 1915 version.

Following this opening, the broad outlines of the 1915 version's 104-bar first movement are the same as those of the final version – again, with a few relatively minor differences here and there – up to just before letter M in the published score. The original first movement concluded with the eight bars shown in Ex. 12. To obtain the sense of this ending, one may begin in the final version's bar 92, the Largamente (3 bars after L), omit the syncopated laments in the winds in bars 93ff, and join up with Ex. 12 at bar 96 (3 before M). The most prominent features of this ending are its two *forte* motivic upheavals in the horn (bars 1–2 and 3–4 of Ex. 12); its two chordal sweeps upward (4 + 4 bars) in the brass and winds (cf. the much earlier passage in the final version, bars 18ff, strings, a passage also present in 1915); its uncompromisingly rugged dissonances; and its inconclusiveness, ending on the weakest possible portion of the bar. Apparently the point was to hear this unsatisfactorily resolved movement as preparatory to the second.

But what of the original movement's 'form' as a self-standing structure? This is an analytical problem that seems particularly acute because of the close (indeed, seemingly inseparable) integration of the two halves of the compound first movement in the final version. Here the answer to the question of form cannot convincingly be found in appeals to the standard *Formenlehre* structures: the relation of the 1915 first movement, *Tempo moderato assai*, to either standard or deformational sonata-practice is anything but clear. It is readily comprehensible, however, within the characteristically 'late-Sibelian' formal and procedural categories outlined in the preceding chapter. In brief, its large-scale structure may be considered as similar to that of the orchestral work composed just before it, *The Oceanides*: expositional rotation / complementary rotation / free, (but, from a larger perspective, 'failed') culminatory rotation (cf. the overview of *The Oceanides*, pp. 28–29 above). This rotational structure will be reconfronted in greater detail in the following chapter.

Separated by a pause from the first movement, the original second movement, *Allegro commodo*, began with explicit echoes of Ex. 11, swaying back and forth on the 'ii⁰₅' of E♭ major in horns and *con sordino* string tremolos,

Example 12. 1915 version, mvmt 1, concluding eight bars

as the beginning of a triple-time scherzo. This gives the impression of a rebeginning, but one that has now come into proper focus or slipped onto the right track. After sixty-four very rapid bars the music tips into C♭ and becomes (with a few minor alterations here and there) the scherzo that we know from the final version's *Allegro moderato* (bar 114, 5 after N). Its 'developmental' section following the Trio (see the analysis in chapter 5) is shorter than that of the familiar version (especially following letter K), and it concludes nearly as abruptly as had the first movement: the extended *più presto* coda of the final version (bars 555ff, 17 after **R**) is absent, and the scherzo ends, somewhat awkwardly, on a weak beat.

The third movement, in G major, *Andante mosso*, is thematically identical to that of the final version's second, but it is shorter (171 bars as opposed to 212) and more obsessively pizzicato, and, most important, its materials appear in a strikingly different schematic arrangement, a full discussion of which, however, would require far more space than is available here. In chapter 5 below I discuss the final version as proceeding through seven successive rotations, the onset of each of which is identified with the appropriate bar number. The easiest way to give a sense of the original version in the brief space allotted here is to map it, after its introduction, with the 1919 rotation numbers:

Ten-bar introduction This begins with 'swaying' high woodwinds alone; the general impression is that given by the horn/woodwind music around bars 41–9 of the final version (beginning eight before **B**). The pizzicato theme itself – an anticipation of the theme proper – begins underneath in the violins and violas with the upbeat to bar 6. (This entry is transcribed in Tawaststjerna, IV, 144.)

First large cycle This is generally equivalent to the music of the 1919 rotations 2/3/4–5 (combination). Roughly considered, it consists of a simpler presentation of the final version's bars 50–108 (from one after **B** to eleven after **E**, but darkened toward its end with a chilling, interpolated E minor chord in the bass instruments, after the counterpart of bar 106, or nine after **E**), skipping immediately to bars 157–73 (from four after **G** to one before **H**).

Second large cycle, mostly identical to the first, but altered at its end This consists of the 1919 rotations 2/3/4 (now with no reference to 5, but, as in the 1919 version, with a retransition at the end foreshadowing in pizzicato the music of Ex. 9 above). Here the general equivalent in the final version is bars 54–124 (from six after **B** to one before **F**).

New, final rotation and formal close (very different from the final version) This new rotation is devoted to a more emphatic statement of Ex. 9, played *poco forte*, and largely in parallel sixths, in the flutes, oboes, and clarinets, a passage that was later suppressed and replaced with entirely different music (from **F** to the end). Toward its end it also suggests aspects of what we would recognize as 1919 rotation 6, especially the passage around the final version's bars 187–93 (2–8 before **I**).

Example 13. 1915 version, mvmt 3, concluding twelve bars

When the first 'large cycle' proper begins (generally similar to 1919's rotation 2, around letter **B**) – by 'large cycle' I mean a structure that itself consists of more than one rotation – the 1915 version presents not the familiar, *arco* quaver variation but a simpler, pizzicato statement of the theme in crotchets throughout. Without question, though, the most important thing to observe about the 1915 'slow movement' is that its two larger, parallel cycles flow into a new, final rotation, in which a seemingly retransitional theme from the end of the second large cycle now *replaces* the pizzicato 'main theme': this is a feature that is not found in the version performed today. As indicated above, this replacement theme, sounded affirmatively in a chorus of woodwinds, is that of the sketch transcribed in Ex. 9. Generating it is the teleological point of the 1915 slow movement's rotations, and, as will be seen, it provides us with a central clue in deciphering the mysteries of the corresponding 1919 movement. For now, though, we need mention only that this 'new theme' serves to present many of the intervals of the subsequent finale's principal theme (cf. Ex. 20, p. 70). Once it is attained the 1915 movement winds down to a close – another inconclusive one, as Ex. 13 shows.

The 1915 finale, *Allegro commodo*, although similar to that of 1919, is more expansive: its 679 bars are subjected to a much clearer, more schematic triple rotation than one finds in the 482 bars of the final version. (And, in fact, as I shall argue in the following chapter, a knowledge of the clearer rotational structure here helps us to understand the somewhat puzzling architecture of the familiar version.) The largest stretch of 'surplus' music – from our perspective – is to be found following the G♭ 'recapitulation', or second sounding, of the Swan Hymn. (In the 1915 version, it should be added, this second sounding was itself twenty-four bars longer than that of the final version.) Here we find a lengthy 'extra' passage of some 119 measures directly before what we now know as the *Un pochettino largamente*. This eventually suppressed passage subdivides into two halves. The first continues the expectant Swan Hymn figuration of the immediately preceding music, *piano* in the rustling strings, and begins before long to anticipate the final 'splitting open' of the theme – the widening of its intervals – which will be sounded climactically (as in 1919) near the movement's end (thus following the principle of teleological genesis). The 'extra' passage's second half recycles portions of what I shall identify in chapter 5 as the third, retransitional section of expositional rotation 1 (1919 version, bars 213–79, beginning eight before G, often heard as a 'development' of sorts), although it is recast here, at the end of complementary rotation 2, in woodwind triplets. (Tawaststjerna transcribes some of this in IV, 145.) Once the slower, E♭ minor passage is reached – the equivalent of letter N in the printed score, which in the 1915 version clearly marks the onset of the third, culminatory rotation – the music is similar to that of the final version, but the crucial events are unfolded at a somewhat slower rate.

Apart from this issue of 'extra sections' we should also mention some of the 1915 finale's local details that differ markedly from those of the final version. The woodwind (later string) counter melody accompanying the first appearance of the Swan Hymn earlier in the movement (beginning twelve before E in the printed score), for instance, is generally different from, and certainly simpler and less melodic than, those in the version that we know. (The opening portion of the original counter melody here is transcribed in Tawaststjerna, IV, 144.) In 1915 the familiar counter theme appears only with the *second* sounding (second rotation) of the Swan Hymn – where its appearance is very much as one finds it fifteen before M in the printed score. This is the theme, of course, that turns into the important E♭ minor *Un pochettino largamente* to follow, and thus in the 1915 score it is an idea that is first only suggested in rotation 1 and is then further shaped and fully attained in its subsequent appearances. The characteristically Sibelian, step-by-step teleological genesis of this theme is a striking, and highly effective, element of the 1915 version. In contrast, the threefold reiteration of the theme in the 1919 finale seems more symphonically 'traditional' – or at least more architecturally symmetrical.

Another local difference that stands out in high relief is the appearance of the *last* counter melody to the Swan Hymn, whose first phrase corresponds to bars 429–32 of the final version (beginning six before **P**). In 1915 Sibelius wrote an achingly 'dissonant' counter phrase in the upper strings – a bold and magnificent touch, unfortunately altered in the later versions – that is nothing less than a slowly played reprise of the first movement's 'second theme'. This is the 'Neapolitan' theme (see Ex. 16, p. 63), and its pitches here in the 1915 finale, f♭³–d♭³–b♭²–a♮²–b♭² (see Tawaststjerna, IV, 146), pull movingly at the E♭-grounded Swan Hymn below, while simultaneously calling our attention, here at the end, to the finale's roots in the first movement. (It should be added that anticipations of this 'Neapolitan theme' had also intruded, much more disturbingly, into earlier portions of the finale in urgent, held-note trumpet dissonances – for example, at the end of the first sounding of the Swan Hymn, after the splendid stretch from E♭ into C major. Usually with puzzled disapproval, or even shock, these splashy intrusions have been mentioned – but not motivically identified – by virtually all prior commentators on the 1915 version. The three-note, *forte* trumpet entry at the C-major end of the first Swan Hymn (the equivalent passage is around letter **F** of the score as eventually printed), d♭¹–a♭¹–g¹, is transcribed in Tawaststjerna, IV, 145, who calls the effect 'almost bitonal'.) Still another important local difference in the 1915 finale is that the famous empty gaps in the set of final chords are filled by long-held chords played by virtually the full orchestra, with tremolo strings, in *crescendo* (IV, 146).

As an architectural whole the 1915 version divides down the middle with two movements on either side. The inconclusive first movement is preparatory to its recasting in the more emphatic second. Similarly the third movement, also inconclusive, is assigned the task of generating the finale's principal theme. Thus as the first movement is completed in the second, so the third is completed in the fourth. More broadly, the preparation-fulfilment model is applicable to the two symphony halves as well. The intervals, thematic shapes, timbres, and so on, of movements 1 and 2 represent a preparatory stage of idea generation that is fulfilled in the movement 3–4 complex. This is surely why Sibelius had ended the second movement, the scherzo, so abruptly (that is, in order to avoid a definitive close); and this is why the first and second movements' 'Neapolitan theme' returns so prominently in the fourth (as an indicator of the grand span of the whole).

The 1916 version

After the premiere of the Fifth, Sibelius's thoughts turned toward its publication. On 5 January 1916 he noted, 'These days I've been working on the symphony to get it into publishable form.' But by mid-January he began to have serious doubts. From his diary on 17 January: 'A terrible counter-reaction after all this. I am still not satisfied with the symphony's form.' 24 January: 'I'm working on the Liebeslied for the violin as well as, secretly, on the new version of the symphony.' 26 January: 'I'm ashamed to say it, but I'm again working on the Fifth Symphony. I am wrestling with God. I'd like to give my new symphony another, more human form. Something closer to the earth, something more alive. The problem was that during the course of the work *I* have changed.' (IV, 158–60) 2 February: 'I'm getting my hands into the reworking [literally, 'retilling'] of the Fifth Symphony!! It hurts, but it hurts sweetly.' (IV, 163)

After mid-February we hear nothing about the revision for about eight months: Sibelius seems to have put it aside in favour of writing smaller, potentially more lucrative works (such as the incidental music for *Everyman*), as well as sketching out some of the earliest stages of the Sixth Symphony and 'planning new orchestral works, with voice or without (?): fantasies or . . . ?' (11 February; IV, 163). Toward the end of the year more celebratory, all-Sibelius concerts were planned for December in Turku and Helsinki, and it was with these in mind that the composer returned to the symphony. In an undated diary entry from the end of October, we finally read, 'I'm working on the new version of the Fifth Symphony. And again I'm in a hurry. But it has to be finished.' On 9 November he writes, 'First three movements at the copyist's (since 4 November). . . . I'm working on the finale'; and on 24 November 1916 he announces, 'The symphony's reworking completed.' (IV, 192)

Sibelius conducted the premiere of the 1916 revision on his fifty-first birthday, 8 December, in Turku; six days later, on 14 December, he conducted it in Helsinki. This is the version of the Fifth about which the least is known. No full score for it survives, and the only completely preserved source of information about it is a single double-bass part now located in the archives of the Helsinki City Orchestra. It should be added, though, that portions of the other orchestral material for the 1916 version also survive, although this material was heavily corrected in order to be re-used for the first performances of the 1919 revision. (Pages were cut out and replaced, passages rewritten and pasted over the originals, and so on: see IV, 50–1). Tawaststjerna is the only scholar who has examined all of this material, and he provides the fullest picture of the 1916 version that we have.

Without a doubt Sibelius's most important revision in 1916 was the suppression of the last few bars of the first movement and the first sixty-four of the second in order to connect the two movements with a climactic bridge. It appears that the 1916 version of this bridge was essentially the same as that of the final version, bars 97–113. This consists of an unforeseen, rapid intensification and immediate plunge into the music of the original opening of the symphony (Ex. 11), only now situated on 'B major' and grandly scored for full orchestra, led by the brass. Emerging so unexpectedly out of the preceding music, the effect is one of the sudden opening of a vast new space – a 'breakthrough' into the scherzo, now labelled *Allegro moderato (ma poco a poco stretto)*. (From his remarks on 9 November, we may infer that Sibelius regarded the result as two movements connected by a bridge; by 1919 he would consider it a single movement.) In a related revision Sibelius altered the beginning of the work by adding the important two-bar 'incipit' in the horns (essentially the present bars 1–2, although the harmonization may have differed slightly; his sketches contain several versions of these two bars), and at this time he probably also revised the subsequent bars to include the feint toward 'B major', as in the present bars 12–13. He also added the *Più presto* coda to the end of the scherzo, which both provided more balance for the whole, larger structure and rendered the ending less inconclusive than it had been in 1915. Thus the overall musical process that resulted – whether we think of it as one movement or two – was now similar to that of the final version: 475 bars as compared with the 1919 version's 473.

The 'third' movement of the 1916 version (that is, the movement with the pizzicato theme) is the most difficult to reconstruct. From the surviving double-bass part we may learn that it had 199 bars (28 more than in 1915; 13 fewer than in 1919) and that its arrangement of material was closer to that of the 1915 version than to the version we know today: in any event, as in 1915 the 'rhapsodic' sections (rotations 3 and 4, in G and Eb) each came by twice, although the second time around they were separated by new, intervening material; the Swan Hymn was still unsounded at any point in the bass; and the whole movement still led to the crucial replacement theme based on

Ex. 9. Its concluding bars, however, were more clearly cadential than those of Ex. 13.

The finale was also substantially different from either version. It was the longest finale of the three, with its 702 bars, 23 more than in 1915 and 220 more than that of the eventual 1919 finale. The most substantial alteration was undertaken at the onset of the third, culminatory rotation, which in the 1915 version had been marked by the slower, E♭ minor episode. At this point Sibelius removed entirely the minor-mode *Largamente* theme (the equivalent of the current bars 407–26) and replaced it with 125 bars of an apparently scherzo-like Vivace, 2/4, in E♭ major, the details of which are not known (IV, 386). This is a puzzling recomposition from our perspective, since the slow E♭ minor theme, anticipated by the woodwind obbligatos over the Swan Hymn, had served the important function of initiating the climactic, final phase of the movement. Whatever Sibelius's motives might have been in interpolating this curious Vivace, it rejoined the 1915 version at the *Largamente assai* (now even closer to its familiar version, bars 427ff, the climactic return of the Swan Hymn). And its end (the passage comparable to the *Un pochettino stretto* of the final version) concluded even more broadly than had the 1915 version.

The 1919 version

Much to Sibelius's distress the 1916 version received mixed reviews from the Helsinki critics. In the Finnish-language press Leevi Madetoja and Evert Katila, writing for the *Helsingin Sanomat* and the *Uusi Suometar*, had praised the new work, but Sibelius's perennial adversary 'Bis' in the Swedish daily *Hufvudstadsbladet* criticized virtually every aspect of the piece: he especially singled out the pizzicato movement, which he had found tiresome, and the conclusion of the finale, which had struck him as indulging unpleasantly in exaggerated dissonances (IV, 194–5). Even Carpelan's 'Swan Hymn' letter from Turku on 15 December 1916, generally brimming over with glowing praise, expressed reservations about the Andante: 'Just a little bit of rhythmic variation here and there and this movement would also have been perfect – this is what your humble friend thinks. The violins' pizzicati seem, perhaps, monotonous.' (IV, 195)

It is no surprise, then, that Sibelius turned again to revising the work as 1917 began, initially with the thought of preparing it for an approaching performance in Stockholm. But by 6 January he wrote to Armas Järnefelt and, in effect, withdrew the Fifth from circulation once again: 'I am deeply unhappy. When I composed the Fifth Symphony for my fiftieth birthday, time was very short. The result was that during this last year I've gone back to it and revised it, but I'm not satisfied. And I *can not*, unequivocally can not, send it off.' (IV, 204) The remark in his diary six days later is bleaker: 'I have to forget [the Fifth]. And I have to go on working. Maybe the sun will shine once again. . . . My soul is sick. And it looks like this is going to last a long time. How did I end up here? For many reasons. The direction of my composing has led me into a blind alley. . . . I didn't make it around the cape.' (12 January, IV, 204)

At this point it seems that Sibelius stopped working on the Fifth Symphony for some thirteen months. During this period the Russian upheavals of 1917 shook Finland to its core. About a month after the Bolshevik Revolution, on 6 December 1917 – two days before Sibelius's fifty-second birthday – Finland was able to proclaim itself an independent republic. By late January and early February 1918 the politically tense country was plunged into a fierce civil war pitting the socialist Red Guards, who controlled most of the south of Finland, including Helsinki and Sibelius's Järvenpää, against the liberal-bourgeois Whites – whose cause the composer deeply supported. By mid-April the Whites, under Mannerheim, would prove victorious. But even as Sibelius's home, Ainola, was being occupied by the hostile Red Guards ('"Forbidden" to go outside [my property] to stroll', he noted in amazement on 5 February 1918: IV, 271–2), he was turning again to his separate, redemptive world of symphonic composition. He was now brooding on a Fifth, Sixth, and Seventh simultaneously, and the contrast here between the harsh external events and this 'unrealistic' interior contemplation could not be more stark.

It was during this period that he decided to revise the Fifth more radically. On 13 January 1918 he noted that he had been working on 'a new E♭ [changed to 'E'] major symphony. Nothing of the old Fifth in it.' On the 18th, he wrote of work with 'the first movement of the Sixth Symphony, E major [*sic*].' (IV, 265) Exactly what this music was cannot be certain, but at the height of the Civil War, on 9 February, we suddenly read in the diary: 'Since yesterday I've been working on the first movement of the Fifth Symphony, which has nothing to do with the earlier [version].' (IV, 272) In short, it seems that between February and May 1918 Sibelius was proposing to uncouple the original first and second movements and to remove entirely the controversial Andante with its pizzicato theme. Thus from his curious, often-quoted letter to Carpelan, who was now gravely ill, on 20 May 1918:

Today's work is the Fifth Symphony in its new form, almost completely recomposed. The first movement is totally new. The second recalls the old one. The third brings to mind the ending of the old first movement. The fourth movement, the old motives, but developed in a leaner, firmer way. The whole, if we can call it that, is a vital rise to the conclusion. Triumphant. (IV, 288)

In the same letter – which, in addition, sets out plans for the Sixth and Seventh Symphonies – we also find the telling remarks: 'From everything I notice how my inner being has changed since the period of the Fourth Symphony. And these symphonies of mine are more confessions of faith than are my other works.' (IV, 290)

Surely a response to prior criticism of the 1915 and 1916 versions, Sibelius's new plan for the Fifth (which he would ultimately discard) seems clear enough, and, curiously enough, it seems not entirely unrelated to his original, late-1914 four-movement plan for the work (as suggested in Ex. 2 above). Restated: the new first movement was probably that E♭/E music mentioned in January 1918 in connection with the Sixth (at present the most reasonable conjecture is that it might have been related to the first-movement music of Exx. 2α and 3),[11] and it was probably separated from the second movement by a pause. The scherzo remained much the same (cf. once again the late-1914 plan), but, of course, it no longer recycled materials, or at least as many materials, from the first movement. The third movement appears also to have been quite new, or at least largely so (could it have been grounded in Ex. 2ε?), although it did contain passages based on the *forte e patetico*, *Largamente* music from the conclusion of the 1915 version's first movement (final version, c. bars 92–7): this would mean that all the preceding music of the 1915 first movement, most of it thematically related to the scherzo, was suppressed. The finale, now shorter, was to end with less of a thematic sprawl, and it was still to rise, via the process of teleological genesis, to the triumphant Swan Hymn at its conclusion.

Sibelius held to this new plan for some time. On 28 May 1918: 'I have worked on the [new] first movement of the Fifth. Yet again. It must become [something] good. Surely the "grip" [holding it together] is under the sign of the "classic". But the motives require it.' (IV, 290) 3 June: 'Will [my classical direction] still interest anyone? It stands apart from today's taste, which Wagnerian *pathos* has influenced, and which seems for that reason theatrical to me and anything but symphonic.' And on 7 June, after confronting a 'psychoanalytical' discussion of aesthetics in the *Finsk Tidskrift*: '[The Freudian theorists] don't realize that a symphonist aspires to strengthen the laws of musical material for eternity.' (IV, 293–4) But once again, at this point he dropped the 'new' Fifth for several months.

Sibelius was prodded into his final burst of activity on the Fifth by a series of moving death-bed letters from Carpelan in early 1919 – letters that affected Sibelius profoundly. On 14 February Carpelan asked the composer about the 'new' Fifth, which, clearly, he believed he would never be able to hear. He wondered in particular about the music that had replaced or revised the 'andante (pastoral)' that he had indeed found 'a little monotonous'; but, with a tinge of regret, he added meekly, 'otherwise I was also very delighted with the first movement (now revised, as you said)'. (IV, 322–3) This almost nostalgic reference to the earlier versions of the Fifth seems to have electrified Sibelius, and he responded with a letter on 23 February 1919: 'In these past few days something great has happened. I regained my sight. The [1916-version] first movement of the Fifth Symphony is among the best things that I have ever composed. I can't understand my blindness. Amazing, that you always supported it. Apparently I've been too close to it or [maybe] my ears have been offended by some impractical, "bad" notes for certain instruments.' (IV, 324) Carpelan responded on 27 February with more words of caution about the 1916 slow movement ('It seemed to me that some slightly long-winded parts had slipped into the second movement') but tellingly added, 'To tell the truth, I was a little frightened when you said you had written a new first movement, but I didn't want to object to it.' (IV, 324–5)

At least in part as a tribute to his dying friend, Sibelius resumed work on the Fifth in late February and March 1919. He now abandoned his 1918 plans for a radically new Fifth (it is unclear what happened to that 'new' first movement; did it become part of the Sixth or the Seventh?) and reverted back to the 1916 version – the one that had so impressed Carpelan in Turku. His primary tasks were thoroughly to rework the 'monotonous' pizzicato-movement and to tighten up the finale's conclusion, something that he had already been thinking about in 1918. On 22 March 1918 he wrote to Carpelan, 'I'm composing new works. Today, the last movement of the Fifth. The arc is on the rise again! It's snowing outside – but spring is showing through it. The willows have changed colour. Life is awakening. This life that I love so infinitely: and this is the feeling that must leave its mark on everything that I compose. Don't give up!' (IV, 326) Two days later, on 24 March, Sibelius received the news of Carpelan's death. He was devastated: 'Now Axel is being lowered into the cold breast of the earth', he noted on the 29th. 'It seems so deeply, deeply tragic! For whom shall I compose now?' (IV, 326–7)

There seems little question that it was Carpelan's death that spurred Sibelius, in his grief, finally to bring to a close his work on the Fifth Symphony (whose premiere he would conduct in Helsinki about seven months later, on 24 November). Indeed, he seems to have thrown himself into the task at once, as if to carry out Carpelan's last request: Tawaststjerna notes a telling lack of entries in the composer's diaries for the next month. But finally we read:

22 April. The Fifth Symphony, *mirabile*, not to say *horribile, dictu*, is finished in its final form. I have struggled with God. My hands are trembling so that I can barely write. . . . Oh, Axel isn't alive! He thought about me up to the very end. Outside +2° and sun. The lake still frozen over. I haven't seen any migratory birds except for the wild geese. But no swans. (IV, 328)

At the last moment – doubtless recalling Carpelan's hesitance to embrace the second movement – Sibelius was once again assailed by radical doubts, and he impulsively decided to lop off two-thirds of the work. On 28 April he wrote:

I removed the second and third movements from the symphony. The first movement is a symphonic fantasia, and it does not tolerate any continuation. My whole work has been based on this!!! Shall I give it the title Symphonie in einem Satze or Symphonische Fantasie: Fantasia sinfonica I? (IV, 328)

Once again we come across the essential generic problem which he had been addressing since he began to compose the piece: 'symphony' or 'fantasia'? But this extraordinary notion of drastically curtailing the work lasted only a few days. All was restored on 6 May 1919, the date of his last diary entry concerning the work's composition:

Rubbish! . . . The symphony will stay in its original three-movement form. All the movements are [now] at the copyist's. . . . Confession: I reworked the entire finale once again. Now it's good. But, oh, this wrestling with God. (IV, 328)

Sibelius, then, could not bring himself to release this work in a version that lacked its *telos*, the finale's grand theme that in 1916 Carpelan, surely echoing the composer, had called its 'swan hymn beyond compare'. His decision to reinstate the last two movements was happily confirmed by an ecstatic sign from the surrounding nature at Järvenpää. According to Santeri Levas: '[Sibelius] never forgot a phenomenon of nature he experienced just when he had put his pen to this score for the last time. Twelve white swans settled down on the lake, and then circled his home three times before flying away.'[12]

Musical process and architecture:
a proposed overview

The Fifth Symphony's local details become clear only when considered within the workings of a single purpose being pursued throughout all of the movements. This is a truism for grasping symphonic works in general, but nowhere is it more critical than in this work. Here the sheer burden borne by the ideas demands such an approach, for these ideas are now claimed to generate the non-normative, *ad hoc* architecture ('content-based form'). If we wish to perceive these unconventional aims, it can be useful to leave some of our conventional expectations behind.

One may consider the symphony's tonal planes, for instance, as slow, 'proto-minimalist' transformation processes. As a whole the work may be heard as a prolonged Eb-major sound sheet set into hierarchies of surface and subsurface motion – as a vast reflection on the symphonic sonority (*Klang*) of the Eb tonic chord. This is the centre of gravity, from which colouristic excursions onto secondary (non-dominant) sonorities are launched, but back into which they inevitably fall. Sibelius illuminates the symphony with only five 'tonal colours': Eb, G, B, C, and Gb. In the first movement the gravitational centre, Eb, is attracted to two other secondary sonorities whose roots are a *major* third above and below, G and B (thus equally dividing the octave by major thirds). G colour re-emerges to govern the second movement. Eb returns decisively in the finale, in which the composer also shifts it, complementarily to the first movement (and narrowing in on Eb), to two sonorous colours whose roots are a *minor* third below and above, C and Gb.

The non-tonic excursions are not so much modulations into new keys as broadly conceived, neighbour-note colour-shifts around members of the Eb triad. Although the specifics are more complex, Ex. 14 suggests the type of semitonal shifting that produces the first movement's supposed G major and B major passages. When they do occur, such tonal planes sometimes initially articulate more or less static $^6_3$ chords. Thus the purported G major of bars 18–30 does not arrive as a self-standing key (something representing a stable root position prepared and defined by a dominant) but as a prolonged $^6_3$

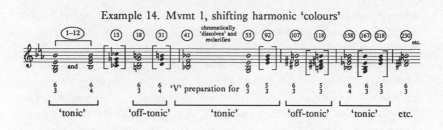

Example 14. Mvmt 1, shifting harmonic 'colours'

sonority above B. Moreover, this $\frac{6}{3}$ is a chromatic inflection of a previously almost-attained B (or C♭) chord (bars 13–17), which itself had been a chromatic offshoot of the movement's initial E♭. Both the B and the 'G⁶' chords are chromatic neighbours of E♭, which is restored by bar 55, again largely through a series of chromatic inflections. This reattained tonic colour will in turn metamorphose into a $\frac{b6}{3}$ above an enharmonic D♯ (bar 107, a shaft of new, intense colour), then underpin that sonority with its B♮ 'root' (bars 118ff) before shifting back to the E♭ tonic, initially in $\frac{6}{4}$ position (bar 158), and so on. Again, a longer-range hearing would interpret all of this as slow colour-transformations in and out of an all-grounding E♭ triad. Gerald Abraham's striking remark about Sibelius's thematic processes in the Sixth Symphony is perfectly applicable to this type of harmonic procedure and, for that matter, to much of the mature Sibelius's musical thought in general: 'The process reminds one of the child's game of altering a word letter by letter, so that "cat" becomes "dog" through the intermediate stages of "cot" and "cog".'[1]

This system of non-dominant-oriented colour-shifts, moving freely between $\frac{5}{3}$, $\frac{6}{3}$, and $\frac{6}{4}$ sonorities, is characteristic of Sibelian harmony, and if we wish to be careful about our terms it can make casual references to presumed 'keys' misleading. For large stretches of the Fifth Symphony Sibelius uses colour-transformations as an alternative to the more powerful, but historically eclipsed tonic-dominant harmony. From this perspective, much of the work is 'about' the difficulty of crystallizing out an unequivocal, successfully functional dominant within such a colour system. This laboured search for what had once been a self-evident, frictionless principle is a prominent aspect of the Fifth's 'historical content'. Had it been composed even ten years earlier, in a pre-Schoenbergian context, much of its sense of struggle would have had a quite different connotation. The final V–I, E♭ tonic cadences of the first and last movements are no mere default conclusions but hard-won victories of tonal clarification. To put it another way, the symphony takes up as a primary topic the difficulty in the period of late modernism of attaining a valid utterance of something (a stable cadence) that in earlier times and earlier 'states of the material' had been simplicity itself. In this sense the symphony may be perceived as simultaneously valedictory and triumphant.

The idea of long-range discovery – slow, rotational transformations toward a stronger and deeper principle – underpins not only the symphony's harmony but also its thematic and motivic materials, its rhythms, and its timbres. The first goal or *telos* toward which the whole work evolves is the finale's Swan Hymn (or 'Swinging Theme'). Its emergence at bar 105 is clearly intended to be revelatory. In its elemental fifths and fourths, its underthirds, its triple hypermetre, its static circularity, its brass timbres (here, horns), and so on, it is produced as the idea to which everything prior had been leading: an implicit essence uncovered. Once fully attained and restated, this first *telos* then permits what had only been potential or transitory to become actual and lasting: it triggers a series of remarkable changes that with great strain effect a permanent shift to the E♭ tonic-dominant principle. Reclaimed from its presumed historical obsolescence, this principle is confirmed in the most direct manner conceivable: the famous widely separated chords of the symphony's concluding nine bars.

Tempo molto moderato (E♭ major)

Actually a fusion of 'first movement' and 'scherzo', the first movement may be regarded as a gradual process that transforms circular weakness or inactivity into linear strength and rapid, forceful activity. In terms of surface energy the movement is a carefully phased *accelerando*. It begins with initial stillness and non-motion – the fermata in bar 2, no accident, is rhythmically thematic – and is drawn by degrees into the whirlwind of its final bars. Harmonically, the movement articulates a similar transformation: an inexorable plunge from the initially weak, recursive harmonic language of its first half into the gravity-forces of the historically problematic cadential language. The trajectory of the whole is that of an end-accented fall that self-destructs, or implodes, both at the point of maximal inner motion (the whirlwind) and also at the point of the strongest cadence.

Formally, the movement has provoked much commentary, and there have been widely differing attempts to analyze it in terms of a freely treated *Formenlehre* sonata. Among the movement's difficult features when viewed primarily in these terms are: 1) the simultaneously single- and double-movement function of the whole structure;[2] 2) its 'double-exposition', in which the second, or 'counter-exposition' (bars 36–71) cycles back from 'G

Example 15. I/1–14

major' to the tonic E♭ and thus seems prematurely to express aspects of recapitulation and resolution as well;[3] 3) its presumed development, which, strictly speaking, is not developmental in any customary textural or harmonic sense; and 4) the uncertainty of determining the precise moment at which the recapitulation begins.[4]

These analytical traps arise when we insist on processing the movement primarily on the basis of what we have come to expect from textbook sonata patterns. Elevating the rotational principle into our primary category, however, and then observing – secondarily – its dialogue with the sonata-deformational principle goes a long way to eliminating these problems. Along these lines the movement as a whole is best described as a series of four broad and increasingly free rotations through a patterned set of materials that may simultaneously be construed as a sonata deformation of the breakthrough type (see p. 6 above). The first two rotations are in dialogue with the tradition of a repeated exposition; the third, and briefest, is a connective passageway occupying the developmental space; the fourth, and longest, beginning with the breakthrough, is based on the recapitulation principle but simultaneously transforms all of the materials into a scherzo with trio and separate development.

Pre-rotational incipit (bars 1–2)

The opening two bars (see Ex. 15) function rhetorically as a proposition setting the tone and terms of what is to follow. To open a symphony with horns – and particularly with the first horn sounding a 'bucolic signal', to use Tawaststjerna's term (IV, 354) – both invokes prior works in the tradition that begin with a similar timbre and invites listeners to recall the poetic connotations of those openings. Such an opening characteristically functioned as a threshold leading from silence, or near silence, into sacred space – vast or magical forests or other nature-places, mystical sunrises, and the like. Consider, for instance, Schubert's Ninth Symphony; Weber's *Oberon* Overture (and the horn quartet near the opening of *Der Freischütz*); Brahms's Second Piano Concerto; the first of Brahms's Songs for women's chorus, horns and harp, Op. 17, 'Es tönt ein voller Harfenklang' (which the Sibelius Fifth – coincidentally? – seems to quote;[5] the 'Morgendämmerung' introduction to Act II, Scene 2 of *Götterdämmerung*; and so on. Related effects would include the sudden 'breakthrough' nature-epiphany in the horns in the slow movement of Mahler's Sixth Symphony (bars 84ff), just prior to the entrance of the *Herdenglocken*, and the second portion of Sibelius's own *Night Ride and Sunrise*. In the symphonic network of intertextuality and self-reference, all compositionally selected sounds, inevitably, have such historical and institutional resonances. In the world of musical modernism there were no neutral materials.

Here the silence is broken with a *piano*, expectant $^6_4$ chord, initially static and non-metric. This 'still sound' expands upward into generative linear intervals and forward into characteristic rhythmic cells. Considered within standard harmonic practice, these two bars recall the normal cadential procedure but 'misfire': Sibelius provides a linear dominant and tonic in the timpani, but no

Example 16. I/20–21

clear $^5_3$ dominant chord emerges above the B♭, nor is the E♭ in bar 2 permitted to support a tonic resolution. This misfired cadence, with its reflective pause, serves at least three harmonic purposes: it measures our distance from the lost world of simple dominants and tonics, made all the more poignant through the fourth- and fifth-orientation of the thematic materials; it produces the sensuous harmonic blur so characteristic of the nineteenth- and early twentieth-century sound sheet; and it sets into motion the succeeding bars, which are cast in the non-goal-directed, recursive language of contemplative oscillation.

Rotation 1, bars 3–35 (referential statement: 'expositional space')

Called into life by the incipit, the work now begins to blossom. Bars 3–10 provide a classic illustration of Sibelian small-scale oscillations supporting 'organic growth'. The eight bars comprise four reiterations of a two-bar harmonic block, the so-called 'ii$^6_5$', here a colouristic upper neighbour to the tonic, and 'I$^6_5$'. This respiration-like motion, swaying back and forth – or in and out of 'E♭' focus – is central to the entire symphony, and the process is rejoined at most of its important moments. Each two-bar call-and-echo block expands its predecessor rhythmically and motivically: the upper-register idea is gradually refracted and shaped into a more profiled 'theme'. By bars 9–10 the thematic idea has grown sufficiently to stride over two bars and attain a dominant. The promised cadence, though, is thwarted in bar 11 (the expected $^5_3$ above E♭ is 'colouristically' replaced by ♭$^6_3$), and the music, still in parallel-third woodwind dialogue, tips toward a blurred, uncertain 'B major' (bar 13).

Everything to this point has been carried out in the 'pastoral' winds, underpinned by timpani. The sudden string entrance in bar 18, *forzando*, *tremolo*, and *poco flautato*, comes as something of a shock. It is as if now the strings, too, have been jolted awake, and instantly the prior potential for B major snaps chromatically into a static 'G^6' (bars 18–27: one hears the ground-sonority with each deep-bass B in the cellos and contrabasses). The harmonic effect of these bars is striking. On the one hand, they are governed by a rock-

Example 17. I/31–7

stable 'G⁶'. On the other, they are coloured by a slow upward, then downward sweep of passing diminished chords in the strings, in its ascent-phase like the lifting of a vast curtain. Woodwind cries ('nature-sounds') emerge immediately above the 'lifting-curtain' sound sheet (Ex. 16): we have entered the second-theme area of the expositional space to which the rotation is alluding. Its opening is insistently dactylic and Neapolitan (A♭) to the 'G⁶'. Thus the principle of the colouristic upper neighbour, which had dominated the first theme, is now intensified and transferred to the second. With its opening fourth-drop and 'circular' two lower neighbours (♭2–♮6–5–♯4–5) this idea also continues to mark the earliest stages of the thematic process that will eventually produce the finale's first *telos*, the Swan Hymn.

Beginning here, Sibelius crafts the rest of the rotation into an end-accented *AA'B* shape (bars 20–23, 24–7, 28–35). Its *B* portion is more energetic and directional than anything heard thus far: with it the composer launches the static 'G⁶' into what is clearly the drive toward a closing cadence. It begins with a more emphatic contour variant of the upward-climbing, 'lifting-curtain' idea, now in both strings and winds and expanding outward with grand exhilaration in both treble and bass. At the moment it reaches its outermost limits (V_3^4/G, bar 30), three low-register trumpets enter in unison, $\hat{5}$–$\hat{8}$–$\hat{5}$ of G, here almost attaining the cadence and simultaneously forecasting interval- and timbre-aspects of the *telos* theme. With this trumpet entrance the entire orchestra has now been summoned.

But now the cadentially directed gears slip. The closing portion of *B* (bars 31–5: see Ex. 17), melodically circular and related to the woodwind cries from *A* (Ex. 16), drops back into the middle register, while its lower voices oscillate through a non-cadential, static voice exchange, one that also declines to confirm the 'G major' implications of what precedes it. Thus although we are deprived of a closing cadence (there has been no cadence at all in the first rotation), we are liberated into a more metric, rhythmically active circularity. The process is now ready to rebegin on a deeper level.

Rotation 2, bars 36–71 (complementary rotation/ 'developmental exposition')

The second rotation is a slightly expanded (thirty-six as opposed to thirty-three bars), varied recycling of the materials of the first. Its 'content' lies in the generative progress that it makes, particularly in terms of momentum and bustling inner activity. Here the tonal motion reverses that of the first rotation. The earlier rotation, that is, had opened up to a new tonal colour (mostly 'G⁶') for the second theme; the second closes back to the norm, E♭ colour (actually 'E♭⁶', above a G bass), at about the same point (bar 54, although the slip back to three flats and the dominant of E♭ at bar 41 is also a decisive moment). This E♭ is then prolonged for the rest of the rotation. The mirror aspect of the two rotations' tonal colours is probably best explained as a function of the grounding principle of circularity or oscillation.

Since the thematic materials return in the same sequence, with about the same amount of attention paid to each (however varied in emphasis and timbre), the second rotation can seem to function as a 'second exposition'. But this interpretation is not without its problems. First, there is no precedent in Sibelius's symphonies for either a repeated or a double exposition. This is a significant objection: already by the later nineteenth century a repeated exposition would have been a profoundly archaic feature, and it cannot be unproblematically invoked here. Moreover, the musical material is significantly altered, and second expositions, however else they might behave, are not supposed to return to the tonic. On the other hand, this rotation does

Example 18. I/102–10 ('breakthrough')

closely retrack the expositional events of the first. Although it is deepened rotation with strikingly different, more active, rhythms, textures, and colours, its thematic ordering seems too neatly and schematically arrayed to be considered a true development (much less an abbreviated development and partial recapitulation).[6] Once again the preferred interpretation would simply declare these *Formenlehre* terminological concerns inadequate. Like its predecessor in *The Oceanides*, this passage is a second, complementary rotation that functions as one of a series of transformations seeking to produce the *telos* at the end of the entire work. In terms of its (doubtless intentional, though secondary) allusions to the formal traditions, it is simultaneously developmental and second-expositional.

Rotation 3, bars 72–105 ('developmental space'/transition)

Essentially a preparation for the breakthrough-transformation that will begin the next section, the third rotation isolates some of the first's individual elements for expansion and variation. This is a developmental procedure that also serves to maintain the secondary dialogue with the sonata-deformational types. The whole passage divides into two subsections, bars 72–91 and 92–105. These correspond roughly to portions of the first and second themes.

The first subsection breaks down much of what has preceded into its most basic gestural parts. This impression of utter reduction – or of entrance into a dark, mysterious passageway – is enhanced both by the lapse into chromatic ambiguity and by the dynamics, which by bar 76 have been choked down to the near-extinguishing point, *ppp*, just as the clarinet and bassoon enter with their mournful, semitone descent. The ensuing, *lugubre* chromatic bassoon wanders for a time through the rustling chromatic murk, but ultimately it moves upward to an E♭ (finally grasping a 'tonic-pitch' crag in the dark passageway). This calls forth a momentary wave of *allargando* brass light (bars 90–92, an 'A♯⁴' chord, *sonore*, with root a tritone away from the E♭ that is still sounded as a bass pedal) in anticipation of the breakthrough to come.

Moving now more deliberately, *Largamente*, and marked *forte e patetico*, the second subsection, implying E♭ colour for most of its course, consists of a series of second-theme-based string pushes toward the breakthrough itself. Marked also by strong, chromatically descending laments in the winds, the first efforts are frustrated and break off. Before long, however, the tumblers click into place, and, *crescendo molto* – but non-cadentially – all now flows inexorably toward the breakthrough in bar 106. This emerges in an epiphany of bright tonal colour, 'B major' (somewhat simplified in Ex. 18 to clarify the harmonic processes), and begins a new rotation.[7]

Rotation 4, bars 106–586 ('scherzo'; 'recapitulatory space')

Within the nineteenth-century sonata-deformation tradition an eruptive 'breakthrough' into the developmental space or at the onset of the recapitulation is a radically destabilizing event after which any sort of default recapitulation becomes inconceivable. Here this opening into a new, brighter vastness brings on a fourth rotation that simultaneously suggests a fundamentally altered recapitulatory process.[8] The four defining 'recapitulatory' features, however – theme, tempo, scherzo character, and 'tonic colour' – are set into place not simultaneously but one after another. This staggering of the recapitulation signals permits a smooth, transitional gliding into the second portion of the movement and blurs our awareness of where any 'recapitulation' might actually begin.

Thematically, the 'B major' breakthrough at bar 106 is a recomposition of

Example 19. I/218–30

the symphony's original 1915 opening (see Ex. 11): it serves as a climactic 'thematic recapitulation' that plugs once again into the 'ii₅⁶–I₅⁶' oscillations – as if into some elemental, generative current. Simultaneously, Sibelius subjects this brief passage to an *accelerando* that drives directly into the 3/4 *Allegro moderato (ma poco a poco stretto)* (bar 114), in which four bars of the new metre correspond to one of the earlier 12/8. By this point the tempo and scherzo character are set in place, but the music is still proceeding in an off-tonic colour, 'B major'.

With the beginning of the scherzo proper (bar 114) – even before Sibelius 'corrects' its colour into E♭ – the 'banished' language of cadences begins to return, doubtless admitted here as part of the resolution function of recapitulation. The first two cadences to appear are weak, in the scherzo's fifth and thirteenth bars (bars 118 and 126), but a more decisive, if still somewhat blurred, cadence is heard shortly thereafter (bars 141–2): this initiates the rocking, unstable passage that will be attracted back to E♭ tonic colour in bar 158. The larger point, then, is that with the 'B major' breakthrough in bar 106 (Ex. 18) Sibelius triggers not only the ensuing recapitulation-scherzo but also makes available once more (albeit on a limited basis) the banished language of cadences, which he will confirm at the end of the movement. With the colour-shift back to E♭ in bar 158 all the elements of the 'recapitulation' are now in place.

As the movement now gains in tonal or cadential gravitational force, its second emphatic cadence, bar 218, launches a 'trio' (Ex. 19) that may be heard as an interpolation affirming the scherzo character of the whole. But any presumed interpolation within Sibelian rotations is always more than that: it is something previously nurtured on a more modest scale and now ready to grow more expansively from within ('teleological genesis'). In brief, the trio is an anticipation of melodic elements of the finale's Swan Hymn underscored here by the return to tonic brass timbre: this is an important stage in the production process of the symphony's *telos*. The theme itself, however, is not yet ready to be stabilized. Sibelius signals this lack of readiness by deflecting it after twelve bars into 'B-major' ($^6_3$) colour (bar 230) and replacing the trumpet timbre with a restatement of the theme in the horns and bassoon. The 'off-tonic' portion of the trio is able to sustain itself as an independent section only until bar 258. At that point it fragments into thematic shards and begins to direct its rhythmic energies toward a retransition (bar 274, the return of the three-flat signature) into the thematic concerns first articulated in rotation 1.

The return to the principle of recapitulation is signalled by the arrival in the violins, bar 307, of the markedly transformed head-motive of the second theme (Ex. 16), now resolved in the tonic E♭. Significantly, Sibelius also expressly associates this theme with the harmonic recursion characteristic of the first theme. This 'recapitulated' second theme appears here over six oscillations of 'I$^6_4$' and the Neapolitan '♭ii$^6_3$' (beginning in bar 298, the actual moment in which the recapitulatory process is rejoined). This recapitulatory passage thus fuses important aspects of the first and second themes. But the E♭ gravitational force is not yet secured. The movement proceeds to spin outward into the tonally shifting thematic bits first heard in the closing section of the trio. By the new, faster *vivace molto* (bar 372) we enter a second interpolated section, an extended, rustling mini-development of fragments that dissolve any clear sense of tonal pull. The very length and seemingly 'gravity-free' chattering of the passage suggest how fragile is the survival, even at this late point, of the E♭ tonic.

Then the grand *coup*. In bar 455 Sibelius reaches into the uncentred fragments to seize control with three unison trumpets sounding the upward-surging incipit motto. This is a forceful *rappel à l'ordre* that reclaims the hegemony of E♭ and triggers the rest of the recapitulation process: now at whirlwind speed, the gravitational principle of dominants and tonics will be powerfully evident. Precipitated into recapitulatory action, the horns try twice to initiate the '*B* portion' of the second theme (bars 471 and, *più forte*, 479). On the third try, in bars 487ff, they succeed, now along with the full complement of winds. This in turn shifts gears into an even faster section, whose brass timbres again foreshadow the finale but, perhaps more importantly, whose furiously rotating bed of strings underneath serves as a recapitulation of the concluding theme of the referential statement (Ex. 17).

A *Più Presto* coda, beginning in bar 555, marks the point of the strongest E♭-major dominant-tonic resolution. In this triumphant conclusion (which, of

Example 20. Comparison of II/108–23 with III/3–23

course, also explicitly recalls that of the much earlier *Lemminkäinen's Return*) Sibelius solidly grasps E♭ as a gravitational key before the rapid speed and sheer cadential force abruptly 'vapourize' into silence.

Andante mosso, quasi allegretto (G major)

Perhaps the symphony's most easily misconstrued movement, the *Andante mosso, quasi allegretto* is the hinge around which its multimovement logic pivots. Although several commentators have been struck by its tone of disarming simplicity – it is not infrequently heard as 'simple and unaffected' or as a space of relaxation between two stronger movements[9] – such an impression misses the mark. Rather, the point is to slip through its intentionally naive, idyllic surface, as through Alice's looking-glass, to encounter the complexities within.

This movement, which harks back to the corresponding movement in the Third Symphony, is often described as a more or less free theme and variations (with 'interludes' or 'transitions'), although Tawaststjerna also heard it as being simultaneously shaped into an *ABA Coda* contour, and Tanzberger, much earlier, had argued that the movement consisted instead of a set of six varied strophes.[10] In the reading offered here the entire movement consists of seven rotations, although it begins *in medias res*, with the concluding portion of an incomplete cycle (called 'half-rotation 0' below) that serves as an introduction. But the movement is less concerned with architecture than it is with process. Its larger purpose is to generate the leading rhythms, metres, timbres, motives, and themes of the finale to come. Once the two incipient finale themes have been produced, the generational sound-matrix that fills most of this movement decays and withdraws. Its function completed, it recedes to make room for that which it has engendered, the finale itself.

To grasp this movement is to focus on the process through which the two thematic goals are generated within the rotations. Goal 1 is the core interval series of the finale's first theme, and it is most unequivocally generated at the end of rotation 4, in bars 108–21 in the pizzicato violins and violas (Ex. 20).[11] Because this thematic point of arrival is concealed within a mid-movement retransition, the contention that it could be considered any sort of goal might at first be greeted with scepticism. Yet, as we have seen, this is the only extended 'slow-movement' passage to be found in the 1914–15 sketchbook (see Ex. 9, a sketch originally intended for a 'Sixth Symphony'), and its key role becomes even clearer in the 1915 and 1916 versions, in which it had been the manifest end-point of the entire movement and was reaffirmed with a woodwind-reinforced repetition. The second idea toward which the movement grows (goal 2) is the finale's Swan Hymn. (The explicit sounding of that theme in this movement occurs only in the 1919 version.) This appears most unequivocally in the contrabasses, *pizzicato*, below the main theme in bars 129–33, a few bars into rotation 5. The central elements of both goals, however, are being continuously shaped at virtually all points of the process. Hearing this happen is the main challenge of the movement.

Half-rotation '0', bars 1–13 (introduction)

As in the first movement, we begin with mixtures of slow-moving woodwinds and horns – the unfolding of the *Klang* backdrop that will generate the principal ideas of this movement. In retrospect, we may understand its events to correspond with those of the concluding portion of the subsequent first rotation (bars 33–45). In other words, the introduction gives the impression of 'tuning into' a more elemental rotation midway through its cycle. From a

Example 21. II/13–47 (upbeat and rotation 1)

broader perspective, then, the theme in the flutes, bars 10–12, concludes a half-rotation, although in the immediate context it impresses also as an initial gesture. The flute theme is simultaneously a closing and an opening.

Rotation 1, c. bars 14–47 (referential statement)

The rotational pattern begins with the theme proper (Ex. 21).[12] In its various slow-movement guises this is almost certainly a recomposition of portions of 'The Harp' from Sibelius's earlier Incidental Music to Strindberg's *Swanwhite* (1908).[13] It consists of an expanded α portion (pizzicato strings), with internal repetition (bars 14–20), and two statements of the subsequent β portion (bars 21–4/25–8; 29–32/33–6), a period with a four-bar antecedent (here, in the flutes) and a parallel consequent (here, in the pizzicato strings). The second β-consequent, however, does not cadence but shifts instead onto a deceptive-cadence 'vi' (bar 36). Here it remains, moving in circular patterns, until it is 'hoisted' back to the tonic (bars 39–40). This leads to an affirmational, concluding repetition of a form of α (here still in the pizzicato strings, bars 43–7). Thus the referential pattern, in shorter terms: α / β antecedent-consequent / β antecedent-consequent / 'vi' / 'hoist' / α.

Example 22. Sketch for the Fifth Symphony (Kilpeläinen, A/0339)

The point is not merely to tick off the themes as they pass by but to concentrate on them as goal-generators. Adequately 'hearing' the α and β themes is recognizing them as upper-voice counterpoints to an as yet unsounded, lower-voice Swan Hymn (or 'Swinging Theme'). As such the principal themes stand for the more important, potential *telos* theme yet to be heard. So much is made clear by some of Sibelius's thematic and revision sketches, one of which is transcribed in Ex. 22.[14]

Once this is understood, several other aspects of the first rotation (and later ones as well) become clearer. The generally parallel underthirds of the β-antecedent in the flutes (bars 21–4; 29–32, not included in the example), for instance, and even more tellingly those in the horn-pairs glowing warmly underneath, foreshadow the underthirds in the finale's first sounding of the Swan Hymn. The horn timbre itself also points toward that moment of the finale, as do the many elemental fifths that sound between the backdrop and the foreground themes. Moreover, the deceptive-cadence 'vi' (bars 36–8) and subsequent thematic 'hoist' through the leading-tone may be heard as helping to generate the $\hat{6}$–$\hat{7}$–$\hat{8}$ aspect of the last movement's grand theme ($\hat{1}$–$\hat{5}$–$\hat{1}$; $\hat{7}$–$\hat{5}$–$\hat{7}$; $\hat{6}$–$\hat{5}$–$\hat{6}$; $\hat{7}$–$\hat{5}$–$\hat{7}$, etc.).

Toward the end of the 'hoist' (bars 41ff) Sibelius begins the G-tonic, high-woodwind, swaying background accompaniment that will pervade rotation 2 and characterize much of the sound world of the rest of the movement.[15] This anticipatory overlapping from the second rotation-to-come dovetails the two rotations and blurs the break between them. Once again, there is a larger generative point here. By stressing the 'lydian' #$\hat{4}$ lower neighbour to 5, c#³–d³ (almost as a separate 'sound of nature'), Sibelius nurtures embryonically some of the defining intervals of goal 1. Compare, for example, the circled

Example 23. II/47–55

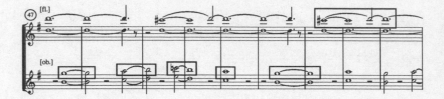

pitches of Ex. 23, taken from bars 47–55 (moving into rotation 2) with the intervals in Ex. 20 above.

Rotation 2, c. bars 47–71 (subdivision into quavers)

The overall pattern of this first 'variation' is: α / β antecedent-consequent / 'vi' / α (as V⁷, prolonged) / new 'closing figure' (darkening onto the minor dominant). Following the example set in the first movement, this one has begun in near stasis and now germinates into more rapid activity. Thus the *Andante mosso* is already starting to be pulled toward the *Allegro molto* of the finale to come. Reflecting this intensification, the upper strings have grown from their initial silence and through the pizzicatos of rotation 1 into a more florid arco melody. The 'vi' and subsequent α serve to release seven soundings of an oscillating C–d figure in the timpani (bars 63–71) along with an important sequential underthird figure in the paired oboes (bars 64–5). Both of these may be heard as shapings of elements that will eventually produce the Swan Hymn.

Rotation 3, bars 72–97 (rhapsodic growth of rotation 2; G major)

Now with pungent cross-relation dissonances against the lower-neighbour appoggiaturas in the oboes ($\hat{7}$–$\hat{8}$ and the 'lydian' $\sharp\hat{4}$–$\hat{5}$), the arco principle unfolds further. The pattern: new 'rhapsodic' incipit (expanding the α-tetrachords into a cascading scale, partially sounded with underthirds) / α (with rotation 2's subdivisions) and its antiphonal repetition / β antecedent-'consequent' (proceeding no further than V⁷, on which it spins its wheels for several bars in 86–97) / 'closing figure' (darkening into G minor). Goal 2 is very nearly generated in the bass under α and the β-antecedent, bars 78–87. Moreover, in the insistently repeated, *rinforzando* D dominants in the horns in the 'spun-wheels' passage one may hear, against the G tonic, the elemental $\hat{1}-\hat{5}-\hat{1}$ of the finale's second theme trying to emerge.

Rotation 4, bars 98–124 (free, 'climactic' restatement of elements in rotation 3 and retransition; goal 1 attained; 'E♭ lydian').

This freest of the rotations ('rhapsodic' incipit / free α continuation / retransition – goal 1) plunges into a significantly contrasting, darker tonal colour, a shadowy space reinforced by potent *crescendo* ascents in the horns and, at least in the initial bars, by the slightly slower tempo (*tranquillo*). Tonally, the implied $^5_3$ (D♮–B♮) over the preceding G-tonic bass has shifted to a $^6_3$ configuration (E♭–B♭). Since there is no 'root-position' E♭ chord in the rotation, the passage may be heard primarily as a colouristic inflection of the G tonic that rules the whole movement. (Notice also, for instance, that the opening melody outlines a G-minor, not an E♭, scale.) Still, as the change in key signature suggests, Sibelius was also touching on 'symphony-tonic' E♭ implications here, and the G/E♭ juxtaposition that emerges, however ambiguously, parallels that of the preceding movement's first two rotations, just as the persistent As in this section push toward the 'lydian fourth' that will help to define goal 1. This 'E♭ lydian', then, both looks back to what has already been heard and is pulled forward by that which is to come. With the various implications now stretched to their utmost, Sibelius proceeds to sound the clearest statement of goal 1 but conceals it within the guise of a retransition (Ex. 20). This ultimately sweeps away the three-flat ambience by slipping to a $^6_4$ over D (bar 125) and the clearer G major of the next rotation.

Rotation 5, bars 125–81 ('expanded' rotation; quasi-reprise and return to G major; attainment of goal 2)

The tempo now accelerates, *poco a poco stretto* (as if drawn toward the finale tempo) up to the *ritenuto* in bar 154. Both the move back to G and the return to a more normally patterned rotation (α / α (expanded) / β antecedent-consequent / β antecedent-consequent / (sharp *ritenuto* into) 'vi substitute' with a new continuation) give the impression of a reprise, but the matter is somewhat more complicated. The crucial point is that once goal 2 has been produced in the bass, bars 129–33, the essential functions of this movement have been completed. Both finale themes have now appeared, and the generational matrix that engendered them begins at once to decay. In the next bars, 134–7, both the theme and its G major become momentarily unstable. The ensuing two statements of β seem to be efforts to shore up the rapidly decaying theme, but each accelerating statement is marked with mixtures from G minor – traces of its death sentence.

The sudden *ritenuto* and move onto a prolonged substitute for 'vi' (now a G chord with added sixth, bars 157–63) suspends the forward motion, while the timpani repeatedly sound the $\hat{1}$–$\hat{5}$ oscillations of the finale to come in a *pianissimo* ecstasy of near-arrival. What follows with the sudden gleaming of the *marcatissimo* pizzicato strings doubled by flutes (actually an expanded recomposition of the earlier 'hoists' from 'vi') is a crisis of continuation. In the 1915 version the suddenly eruptive, 'polychordally' discordant, and *fortissimo* ascents in the brass and winds (in the final version, bars 167–9 and 173) had appeared much earlier, before the appearance of goal 1. There they had had the clear effect of a command to 'Go back!' – to recommence a da capo cycle of rotations that would eventually be more successful in producing the desired goal-theme. In the final version the command seems to signify something like 'Go no further! Your work is done!', and, significantly, it is followed by a fermata. Subsequently, however (bar 174), the α motives do peek out, as if to plead for – and ultimately to obtain – permission to complete a minimal rounding of the movement in rotations 6 and 7.

Rotation 6, bars 182–97 (decayed rotations 1/2)

With continued minor-mode decay, rotation 6 fuses a portion of rotation 1 (bars 182–7 = 29–34, with the flute timbre now changed to that of a poignant oboe cradled by first-movement-like tremolo oscillations in the strings, expressing 'D$_2^4$') with the concluding bars of rotation 2 (195–8 = c. 64–70, compressed), which recycle such things as the swaying, 'lydian'-appoggiatura backdrop in the upper woodwinds and the 'underthird' figure in the paired oboes. Between them (bars 188–94) Sibelius places a static 'ii$_5^6$' in *decrescendo*, which simultaneously recalls the importance of this chord in the first movement and substitutes for the more normal 'vi' found in the slow-movement rotations.

Rotation 7, bars 198–212 (Poco largamente *valediction*)

Rotation 7 is an expansion of the 'closing figure' first heard at the end of rotation 2 (bars 70–71). This dark-hued, minor-mode 'lake of tears' music serves as a farewell to the movement, whose G major is now riddled with G-minor decay. Perhaps its strongest effect is the gradual clarifying of the minor and the heartfelt substitution of an 'open-air', held 'IV⁶' for the more expected 'vi' in bar 208. The G-major *Tempo I* conclusion in the winds (bars 209–12) attends to the business of proper cadencing. But one might also notice that it seems to allude (intentionally?) to the codetta of the 'Hinterweltler' section of Strauss's *Also sprach Zarathustra*, which was also a fervent 'Leb' wohl!' to a cherished something that had to be given up in order to proceed to a higher level.

Allegro molto (E♭ major)

Somewhat paradoxically, the triumphant finale has proven to be both disarmingly simple and deeply puzzling to commentators. On the one hand, its broad architectural effects, disposed in a succession of massive, repetitive blocks, could scarcely be clearer. The finale tradition to which Sibelius alludes here, as in his earlier symphonies, is that of the finale built from radically simplified materials. This is a tradition particularly dear (but not exclusive) to the nationalists, one in which the 'institutional' sophistication of the initial movement dissolves into more basic or 'naive' ('truer') elements in the finale. Moreover, it has become common to interpret this finale's role within the symphony along the symmetrical rhythm-and-tempo lines proposed and discussed at length by Lionel Pike: 'The overall plan of the symphony resembles an arch – the tempo of the opening movement changes from slow to fast, the second movement combines the two speeds in counterpoint (and at one place in heterophony), and the Finale starts with fast music but ends slowly.'[16]

On the other hand, despite the seeming directness of its architecture and effects, the movement has been difficult to categorize satisfactorily within the *Formenlehre* types, because Sibelius has not treated the large blocks in orthodox ways. Certain aspects, though, seem clearly sonata-like. It has two contrasting themes (the first in E♭, the second beginning in E♭ and then shifting to C) and, after a brief transitional (or developmental) passage, bars 213–79, it restates them in a manifest thematic reprise (beginning in G♭ in bar 280, then moving eventually back to E♭). Thus for Gerald Abraham it is a movement 'following the outline (though not the key plan) of sonata form'.[17] But there are more problems with this presumed sonata than that of an unusual ordering of tonal colours. For example, within the sonata framework it is also difficult to explain why the reprise's second theme, having arrived at its expected end-point (bars 406–7), suddenly shifts its tone to broaden further into the E♭ minor section, *Un pochettino largamente* (bars 407–26). And to relegate the *nobile*, E♭-major return of the Swan Hymn in the trumpets at the *Largamente assai*, bar 427, to the mere status of a 'coda', as is normally done, seems inadequate: this is the onset of the grand *telos*, the moment of clarification toward which the entire symphony has been pointing.

Apparently uncomfortable with sonata solutions, a few commentators, such as Simon Parmet, have suggested that the movement be interpreted as 'a kind of rondo . . . clear and unambiguous . . . main theme – second subject – a short working-out section – main theme – second subject – coda'. The schemes invoked, however, are far from self-evident.[18] Most recently, Erik Tawaststjerna began his analytical discussion of the finale by referring to it as 'rondo-like' but shied away from the problem of elaborating fully the structural details. (They apparently include a sonata-like 'recapitulation of the first theme [that] begins in G♭ major'.)[19] The most idiosyncratic analysis of the movement has been that of Tanzberger, who dispensed with references to either sonata or rondo and heard the movement as a 'strophic form' – a succession of four (or 2×2) strophes, which he labelled *A* (bar 1), *B* (bar 105, the Swan Hymn), *A₁* (bar 213, the return to three flats, more normally considered a retransition or the onset of a short development), *B₁* (bar 360, in G♭ in the strings), and *coda* (bar 427, *Largamente assai*, E♭).[20]

Parmet's, Tawaststjerna's, and Tanzberger's rondos and strophes doubtless emerge from their sense of the overriding circularity of the movement's large- and small-scale gestures. Having developed a category to address this sense, we would do well to consider this movement, too, as primarily an unfolding of a set of broad, teleological rotations. To this end, recalling the processes of the longer 1915 finale is essential (see pp. 49–50 above). There we encountered three explicit rotations, not in a manifest dialogue with any *Formenlehre* scheme – indeed, it was a radically 'Sibelian' structure. The first rotation comprised three sections, all of which were retained in the final version (theme 1, theme 2, and the 'retransition'); the second, complementary, rotation repeated these, with tonal and textural variations, along with some crucial anticipations of the later *teloi*; the third, culminatory, rotation (starting with the equivalent of the *Un pochettino largamente*) concentrated on the second theme and led toward the grand *teloi* proper. By 1919 the longish third section of rotation 2 (the retransition and anticipations) had been entirely removed, but the tri-rotational principle remained intact, if a bit obscured. This is the category, then, in which the movement is most productively understood. Fundamentally, it is a rotational/teleological structure, and its secondary dialogue with the sonata-deformational principle, to the extent that it exists

Example 24. III/52–140, hypermetre (with note-values halved)

at all, is rather tenuous – more so than was the case in the first movement.

Throughout all this one must not lose sight of the movement's larger aims. These are: through deepening rotations to produce the Swan Hymn as a first *telos*; to restate it in an off-tonic colour (G♭), but one properly situated to lead it definitively back to an increasingly stable E♭ major (bar 427); then – most remarkably – to 'crack open' the presumed *telos* itself (bars 435ff) to release an even grander one in a final revelation, prolonged and *fortissimo*, the unshakable regrasping of the 'historically eclipsed' cadential harmony that was initially represented as ungraspable in the first movement's opening two bars.

Equally crucial is to hear the basis of this movement in the material and procedures of its immediate predecessor. As is the case with the two sections of the first movement, the last two movements may be perceived as an indissoluble, complementary pair. As in the 1915 version the relationship of the slow movement to the finale is that of preparation to fulfilment. To reach for a striking metaphor, the finale can impress us as the slow movement pulled inside-out: that which was previously only latent or merely supportive is placed here in the foreground. This includes not only the finale's first and second themes but also certain aspects of timbre and metre. Similarly, several motivic features of the slow movement appear here only as background. An informed listening, then, should call forth the close relationship of the slow movement and the finale. One may even speak of their 'identity', considered in the broadest terms. Together they constitute a single progressive gesture on the way to the first *telos* – and then beyond.

Rotation 1, bars 1–279 (referential statement in three sections; attainment of first telos)

Up to the point of the grand shift into C major in bar 165, the dramatic conclusion of the second theme, the first portion of this movement is a massive, static E♭ block set into inner motion. The point of this broad sound sheet is to permit the urgency of the rapid molecular vibrations of its circular first theme to 'heat up' to the point of igniting the second. Despite the contrasting surface characters of the themes, Sibelius conceives the bithematic complex, nominally 'sections 1 and 2', as a single process: the recovery of a kinetically generative, tonic E♭ that is now prepared to liberate the *telos*-theme in that tonic, then expand outward into a *plein-air* C major.

For our purposes, we need note only that the first idea (see Ex. 20) appears in four successive subrotations on its way to the second theme (bars 1, 26, 62, and 77, vaguely suggesting *fugato* entries). Its first subrotation is introduced in bars 1–5 with the tonic E♭ bounded by fourths on either side (e♭^{1}, b♭, a♭^{1}). These elemental fourths foreshadow the fifths of the Swan Hymn, and the subsequent theme in the subdivided strings freely employs both the 'lydian' $\hat{4}$ and 'mixolydian' $\hat{7}$ to suggest, among other things, an urge to expand the initial measures' boundary-A♭ up to the proper B♭ dominant, a pitch that the *telos*-theme will require for its proper ignition, and then to attempt to circumscribe and stabilize that dominant. Creating a more stable dominant is a central concern of all four subrotations.

Perhaps the most masterly element of the first rotation is Sibelius's treatment of hypermetre (larger metric groupings across the bar line): the gradual undoing of duple rhythms to spring them into triples for the onset of the second theme. The first theme itself begins squarely with a 'strong beat' on every other bar (bars 5, 7, 9, 11, and so forth) – a duple, 2/2 hypermetre – but the first subrotation contains a three-bar descending scale at its end (bars 23–5) before the return to duples for the thematic onset of the second subrotation (bars 26, 28, 30, 32, etc.). Bars 42–51 are capable of differing hypermetrical interpretations, but at least by bar 52 (the attaining of a held dominant in the upper woodwinds), we seem more unmistakably to encounter two three-bar groupings, and the hypermetric transition into the triple-time second theme is now pursued through the unpredictable alternation of two- and three-bar units. Ex. 24, in which the actual note values have been halved and the original time signature altered for analytic purposes, demonstrates one hearing of the hypermetric procedure from bar 52 through bar 140.

Of particular interest is the polymetre that begins with the contrabasses' entrance in bar 99. This is the 'unstable' moment in which duples are definitively abandoned in favour of triples. Treble and bass metres come back into phase in bar 105, the moment that the triple-time Swan Hymn first sounds in the horns. (The D–E♭ downbeat in the bass, bars 108–11, recalls the ascending semitone appoggiaturas that were a prominent feature of the slow movement; thus the bass confirms the most directly generative source of this theme in the prior movement.) After the first subrotation of the circular, twelve-note *telos* we are released into an extraordinary polymetric canon by augmentation. In bar 117 the upper voices (reckoning within the halved note-values of Ex. 24) are probably most properly heard by now as unfolding in 12/4 – the next level of hypermetre above the preceding 3/4. (In the actual notation of the score the implied metre is 12/2.) In the contrabasses below, the 'Swinging Theme' unfolds three times as slowly, in an implied 9/4 (in actual notation, 9/2), although, of course, there is also a broader level of hypermetre in the bass, in which a single hypermeasure would last as long as the sounding of the theme's twelve notes.

Thus at this point one finds the revelation of the cyclical, the intervallic, and the temporal mechanisms that have animated the whole work. Moreover, as the successive horn dyads are sounded, Sibelius lets their pitches ring out in sonorous blurs in the held strings: this is one of the clearest examples of the 'artificial pedal' orchestral effect of which Sibelius was so proud.[21] Once the polymetric canon is securely launched, it blossoms further into an eloquent, upper-voice wind counterpoint (subrotation 3, bar 129, also derivable from materials in the second movement). This counter-theme will be emphasized further in the next rotation, and it will ultimately function as the crucial 'entrance' feature of the culminatory rotation – the preparation of the pathway to the grand *telos* at the work's end. We may also notice that here in the first rotation, in the concluding, slightly longer subrotation 8 – now having stretched out to its radiant C major – the second theme begins 'unstably' to expand its intervals (bars 189ff). This, too, is a crucial moment: while the interval expansion comes to nothing here, it will have important consequences near the end of the movement.

With its sense of a clean break from what precedes it, the first rotation's third section, bars 213–79, seems to be a separately articulated space in its own right. Considering its 'pre-history' in the 1915 version, it is probably best heard as an extended retransition that recycles us into a second broad rotation. Its fragmentary, modulatory quality, however, also tempts us to hear it – secondarily – as occupying a brief developmental space within a sonata deformation. It begins with an immediate restoration of the E♭ tonic colour that had been abandoned only in bar 165, and thematically its opening, bar 213, rejoins material initially heard in the first theme's second subrotation, beginning at bar 55. Within a few bars it develops a new offshoot in a pair of chattering oboes in thirds (bar 221) whose melodic material is traceable to the concluding theme of the *first movement*'s referential statement (bars 31–4, see Ex. 17). The oboes lead the E♭ tonic downward into C minor (bar 242), and a trumpet-bassoon-timpani 'swelling-breeze' blows through the orchestra in order to lift the tonality up to G♭ for a subrotational repetition of the oboe chattering (bar 249). This time the descent leads us into E♭ minor (bar 263). In a concluding block of retransition proper, alternating upward hoists from woodwinds and humming strings return (but not with dominants) to G♭ to deposit us gently, in *diminuendo*, at the doorstep of the next, quasi-recapitulatory rotation.

Rotation 2, bars 280–406 (shortened complementary rotation; first two sections only)

The point of the initial G♭ colour here is twofold: to counterbalance the first rotation's C major and to establish the pitch level that will assure the recapturing of E♭ when the second theme's conclusion makes its expected dramatic shift down a minor third. The off-tonic beginning, the *misterioso* marking, and the muted string section suggest that these 'mysterious workings' mark the arrival of a special corridor bringing us closer to the grand statement of the symphony's true *telos*. The rotation's thematic processes are easily followed and need little comment here. We might note only that the slightly varied first theme is shortened, beginning, in effect, with subrotation 2 from the exposition, and that the hushed arrival in the strings of the Swan Hymn in G♭ is kept remarkably understated throughout its four subrotations: this is a strategic move to bring the woodwind counter-theme into more prominence. (In the 1915 score this version of the theme was first attained here; only a rudimentary form of it – minimally processed nature-cries – had been sounded in rotation 1.)

Rotation 3, bars 407–82 (culminatory rotation; attainment of grand telos)

At the end of the theme's fourth subrotation in rotation 2 we expect it, of course (judging from rotation 1's model), to shift down a third to E♭ major – to initiate, perhaps, a 'tidy' conclusion of the symphony. But Sibelius withholds this resolution and, eliding much material originally present in the 1915 version, moves directly into the culminatory rotation 3. This begins in E♭ minor, *Un pochettino largamente* (bar 407), at which point, with the existing hypermetre now explicitly notated as 3/2, the tactus begins its process of decelerating. Although the previous subrotations of the theme continue here in the woodwinds (subrotations 5, 6, and expanded 7 – thus crossing the rotational 'break' and binding the two together into something of a single gesture), this passage functions both as a second and final corridor on the way to the grand *telos*[22] and as the final apotheosis of the preparatory, 'nature-cry' counter-melody, now taken up rhapsodically in the strings.

All of this is a heartfelt farewell to the now-decaying processes that have been generating the triumphant final goal, now ready to stride forth. Most important, though, at the end of the corridor we find the eloquent laying down of that rare feature in this work, the spotlighted dominant of E♭, in bar 423, followed with its determined, unflinching resolution into the onset of the grand *telos*, the E♭-major *Largamente assai*, in bar 427, *nobile* in the trumpets (and now shorn of some of its underthirds). This regrasping of the historically obsolescing cadential principle within a symphony in which it has been so elusive is one of the strongest effects that Sibelius ever penned. ('One last time', as it were, before the eclipse becomes total: a sense of intense valediction pervades this and everything that follows.)

The *mezzo piano* subrotations 8 and 9 (bars 427 and 431) are capped with two still-muted string 'benedictions' acknowledging that the goal-generating process has now reached the point where its success is secure. What happens subsequently, however, is astonishing. In what amounts to an exploded tenth subrotation (bar 435 – now with unmuted strings) the theme gains energy, *poco a poco crescendo*, and, with great effort, its carefully measured intervals begin to expand. (We should recall that this wedgelike opening of the *telos* was Sibelius's first-sketched plan for this theme and one of the earliest-generated ideas for the symphony as a whole.) Thus we discover here that the 'first *telos*' – the Swan Hymn *qua* 'theme' – has not been the true end-point of the symphonic process. Rather, once secured as a stable, but still 'volitional', sound-object, it now 'opens up' with stress and trembling to give birth to something beyond itself. This is represented by an even more celebratory final cadence, *fff* and *un pochettino stretto*, which ushers in an apotheosis of recaptured, 'orthodox' cadential harmony (bars 467–82), stated in the most direct and elemental way.

Tawaststjerna has pointed out the persistence of 'Swinging Theme' inner-voice motion in the famous widely spaced chords at the end: in a sense they sound one last subrotation of the theme.[23] Equally to the point, though, the essential harmonic progression of the final sixteen bars is I (467), 'IV$^6_4$' (472), 'cadential $^6_4$' (474, literally I^6 at this point, of course, although the listener's attention is clearly drawn to the *ffz* dominant in the timpani – at best, the 'literal' I^6 is something of a substitute for the cadential $^6_4$ at the onset of the spaced chords, which, *Coriolan*-like, must be hammered through in order to move to the 'proper' V), V (prolonged, with inner motion, in bars 476–80, but finally produced 'ready to resolve' in bar 481), and I (482, the final bar). This represents, of course, the harmonic orthodoxy that has been 'historically unavailable' for most of the work. Above all, we should notice that this unique I–'IV'–'cadential $^6_4$'–V–I statement at the end reinvokes the stacked fourths ($\hat{5}$–$\hat{8}$–$\hat{2}$–$\hat{5}$) heard at the beginning of the first movement – the initially 'misfired' cadence that set the whole process in motion. By reinterpreting the stacked fourths more 'harmonically' ($\hat{1}$–$\hat{4}$–$\hat{5}$–$\hat{1}$), the end of the symphony triumphantly gathers up, and then resolves, its beginning.

Editions and performance tempos: a brief note

A relatively recent phenomenon, advanced Sibelius scholarship is still in its earliest phases. Before the currently available editions of the works can be properly assessed and 'critical editions' prepared, when needed – not to mention more complete collections of the letters, diary entries, and so on – a wealth of data scattered in various cities still needs to be uncovered, inventoried, and made accessible. In addition to Erik Tawaststjerna's monumental biography, the central coordinating document of virtually all current thought on the composer, two important recent publications from Finnish scholars have continued the advancing trend of ground-level Sibelius scholarship. Fabian Dahlström's catalogue from 1987, *The Works of Jean Sibelius*, includes much publication and first-performance information. And Kari Kilpeläinen's impressive catalogue from 1991, *The Jean Sibelius Musical Manuscripts at Helsinki University Library*, inventories the largest collection of Sibelius sketches, drafts, early versions, and fair copies in the world. Much (but by no means all) of this huge collection was originally Sibelius's own, accumulated throughout his entire life. These personal manuscripts eventually passed into family hands and thence, in 1982, into the Helsinki University Library. Dahlström's current project at the Sibelius Museum in Turku is the production of an expansive thematic catalogue, which will also provide an overview of the principal printed and manuscript sources of the works. Progress on this catalogue is well under way, and it is hoped that it will begin to make the production of a critical edition possible.

In the interim it is safe to say that in many instances it will be difficult to determine what the base text for a critical edition should be – say, of one of the symphonies.[1] The currently available autograph scores were not always Sibelius's last word on editorial matters. On occasion, for example, he may have prepared more than one 'fair copy' of the scores, one for private possession and one to serve as the *Stichvorlage* proper, and these copies were not always identical. Some of the *Stichvorlagen* on the continent were subsequently lost, or destroyed during the war years. In addition, we know that he occasionally made post-autograph corrections in the proofs and that the manuscript evidence of many of these proof-changes has also been lost. (The notice in Hansen's publications of Symphonies 5 and 7, 'Edited and revised by Julia A. Burt, New York', apparently means little: the Burt 'revisions' almost certainly involved negligible things, but such a notice did permit the publisher to secure an American copyright.) Similarly, Sibelius occasionally decided to alter portions of his works several years after their publication and notified his publishers of this only by means of still-unpublished correspondence, or perhaps only by reporting the changes verbally, as he seems to have done to his son-in-law, the conductor Jussi Jalas. To what extent such alterations are actually 'definitive' – or whether that term really applies at all – will remain problematic.

Because Sibelius normally saw the first-edition proofs of his major works, the available printed editions do possess a certain authority, yet they also contain a few errors and passages that have been questioned. In 1970 Paavo Berglund, invoking the authority of the autograph score, called attention to hundreds of specific discrepancies in the Seventh Symphony in his *A Comparative Study of the Printed Score and the Manuscript of the Seventh Symphony of Sibelius.* Most of these involved the precise placement of dynamics and articulations, but a few were also concerned with wrong notes. The publishers (Hansen) entered these into the 'Revised Edition (1980)' of the Seventh. Berglund's work in the later 1960s and early 1970s also led to apparently less startlingly revised editions of both the Fifth (1974, the first work to be revised) and the Sixth (1981), also published by Hansen. In the case of the Fifth Berglund reports in an informative Preface that he specifically included a 'few additional alterations' that Sibelius had requested of Jalas: for example, in the first movement, bars 90–92 (letter L), Sibelius told Jalas to change *allargando al Largamente* to *un pochett allarg. al largamente.* The most significant, audible change, though, occurs near the beginning of the symphony, in bars 12–17. In the Berglund edition the parallel thirds in the woodwinds in bars 12, 14, and 15 (oboes, clarinets, and oboes again) are maintained only for the first nine semiquavers in each bar, not through twelve, as in earlier editions. Semiquavers ten through twelve now appear in unison, following the earlier version's original top voice. (See Ex. 15 above, which transcribes the older printed edition.) The only edition currently available from Wilhelm Hansen – for the score, the parts, and the study score – is that of Berglund's revision.

To judge from the available evidence, the recorded performance tradition of Sibelius's symphonies may be an inadequate guide to the conception of the works that the composer had in mind. Santeri Levas's recollections on this point merit quotation at length:

It was of the greatest importance to [Sibelius] that his works should be properly performed. If he heard a faulty performance on the radio he would grumble about it for days afterwards. Unfortunately this often happened. 'It is inconceivable how unfamiliar my works continually are to present-day conductors', he wrote to Georg Schnéevoigt. This was as late as 1942 when he had long been world famous. Particularly in countries where his music was beginning to take root, the *tempi* were always wrong. It could happen that a young conductor would take sections twice as slowly as he should have done, but mostly *tempi* were too fast. Sibelius, referring to this, often said that the unrest of the technological age communicated itself to music. 'Composers and conductors of today generally don't seem to know how a real *Adagio* should sound.' . . . He often asked his publisher if he would put in metronome markings for the benefit of the ill-informed conductor. . . .

Even though there were a great number of them Sibelius was always critical of recordings of his works. One evening when this was being discussed, he sighed as he said: 'Actually I have never been completely satisfied with any single recording.'[2]

It would seem that by the early 1940s – long after the publication of the Seventh Symphony (1925) – incorrect tempos in performance had become such a problem that Sibelius drew up a separate list of metronome markings for each of his symphonies. In some instances he wrote these into his own copies of the published scores: for instance, in his personal copy of the Third, now preserved in the Helsinki University Library, one finds such handwritten indications.[3] In any event, it is clear that Breitkopf was notified of Sibelius's wishes, and the complete list for all seven symphonies was published in early 1943 in the Finnish journal *Musiikkitieto* (*Musicology*) under the title 'Metronome markings for the Sibelius symphonies'. Its opening sentence reads: 'A leaflet has been published by Breitkopf & Härtel on which is marked the specific tempos of the composer himself. These metronome markings, of course, show the tempo only approximately.'

In 1950 this information was reproduced in translation and provided with an introduction by David Cherniavsky in an article in *Music & Letters* somewhat misleadingly titled 'Sibelius's tempo corrections'. Moreover, it seems that Sibelius himself had personally lobbied Cherniavsky on the matter of tempos: 'He does not wish [these markings] to be taken too strictly, but only as a corrective measure called for particularly by the recordings of these works. The following list of Sibelius's own metronome marks . . . was brought to my attention during a recent visit to the composer.'[4] Because this important list failed to make its way into either any subsequent editions or any prominent

Table 1. Sibelius's post-publication designated tempos (1942–3)
for the Fifth Symphony

Tempo molto moderato	♩. = 66	
Largamente (p. 25, bar 92)	♩. = 63	
Allegro moderato (p. 30, bar 140)	♩. = 80 ⎤	gradually
D (p. 39, bar 218)	♩. = 96	forward
K (p. 49, bar 372)	♩. = 104	into the
M (p. 52, bar 423)	♩. = 112	next tempo
N (p. 54, bar 447])	♩. = 126 ⎦	
Presto (p. 60, bar 507)	♩. = 138	
Andante mosso [sic]	♩ = 80	
Allegro [sic: not Allegro molto]	♩ = 160	

Sources: 'Metronomimerkinnät', 1943; Cherniavsky, 1950

commentaries, Sibelius's markings have remained little known to this day and have exerted little, if any, influence on the performance tradition of his symphonies. It appears that Sibelius's complaints from the 1940s still hold.

The composer's requested tempos for the Fifth Symphony are reproduced in Table 1. They are perhaps best considered in conjuction with Table 2, a more expanded list of the approximate tempos of seven recordings of the Fifth Symphony: the 'historical' June 1932 recording with Robert Kajanus, Sibelius's associate and former teacher, conducting the London Symphony Orchestra (the first complete recording, originally released on seven 78 sides);[5] Herbert von Karajan and the Berlin Philharmonic (1965, the second of his three recordings of the work);[6] Lorin Maazel with the Vienna Philharmonic (1966, his first recording of the Fifth);[7] Colin Davis with the Boston Symphony Orchestra (January 1975);[8] Vladimir Ashkenazy with the Philharmonia Orchestra (recorded October 1980, released 1981);[9] Paavo Berglund with the Helsinki Philharmonic (the second of his two recordings, recorded December 1986, released 1988);[10] and Leonard Bernstein and the Vienna Philharmonic (similarly, the later of his two recordings, recorded September 1987, released 1989).[11] It should be added that I have selected these seven recordings not as my personal proposals for the 'best' available readings but rather, first, as widely circulated representatives of the tradition; second, as manifesting sharply differing conceptions of the work; and, third, as helping to form a spectrum of differing personal, and perhaps 'national', conducting traditions. Many other prominent recordings do not appear on the list: those

Table 2. Comparative tempos in seven recordings of the
Fifth Symphony (approximate metronomic speeds)

location [bar]	Kajanus (1932)	Karajan (1965)	Maazel (1966)	Davis (1975)	Ashkenazy (1981)	Berglund (1988)	Bernstein (1989)
First movement: *Tempo molto moderato*							
opening [3]	63	48	54	46	46	50	46
second theme [20]	66	48	54	46	52	50	44
second rotation [36]	66	48	66	50	58	60	54
Largamente [92]	60	42	63	38	48	46	40
breakthrough [106]	84	42	60	44	50	54	42
Allegro moderato [114]	88	69	69	69	80	69	60
B, E♭ major [158]	80	84	78	80	92	86	70
D, trio [218]	92	94	92	82	92	94	72
K, Vivace molto [372]	98	106	120	104	120	104	88
M [423]	116	116	130	104	120	108	98
N [447]	116	118	132	108	130	110	100
Presto [507]	112–26	138	142	132	144	134	134
conclusion	138?	148	148	144	148	140	140
Slow movement: *Andante mosso, quasi allegretto*							
introduction [1]	56	76	60	60	66	74	48
flute theme [10]	69	76	88	66	63	78	63
B, rotation 2 theme [49]	80	80	92	66	66	86	66
Poco tranquillo [74]	54	58	80	54	56	74	48
goal 1/retransition [111]	84	88	96	84	76	80	74
Poco a poco stretto [126]	96	108	104	92	104	102	80
Poco largamente [198]	60	56	80	54	50	58	42
Tempo I [209]	52	72	76	56	60	60	46
notable ritard. at end?	yes	no	yes	no	yes	yes	yes
Finale: *Allegro molto*							
first theme (♩) [5]	168	168	192	188	176	168	164
Swan Hymn [105]	144	160	180	176	152	172	148
Un poch. larg. (♩) [407]	58	63	76	80	63	69	50
Largamente assai [427]	54	58	69	60	58	60	48
Un poch. stretto [467]	56	84	72	66	92	78	56

of Koussevitzky (an informative – and excellent – reading from 1940, the second recording made of the work),[12] Collins, Ormandy, Barbirolli, Rattle, Salonen, Järvi, Saraste, and so on.[13]

One might expect the seventy-five-year-old Kajanus's recording – a central constituent of the Sibelius Society's project to commit all of the symphonies to disc – to carry special authority. He was a conductor, after all, who had known Sibelius personally for over forty years and had had a long series of distinguished Sibelius performances earlier in the century. Moreover, Sibelius had (albeit in a manifestly commercial statement) endorsed the conductor's 1930 recordings of the First and Second Symphonies: according to Guy Thomas, the Columbia Records announcement on 30 May 1930 concerning the forthcoming release in 1931 of those recordings had included a statement from the composer that 'no one had "gone deeper" into these symphonies or "given them more feeling and beauty than Robert Kajanus" '.[14] What immediately strikes one upon hearing the Kajanus recording of the Fifth – and what most sets it apart from its successors – is its extraordinarily flexible sense of tempo on the local level, which can be only partially suggested in Table 2. (In the table some of the indicated tempos, especially for the Kajanus recording, attempt to capture general speeds that are actually in transition.) Often eschewing any suggestion of a strict or metronomic beat, Kajanus kneads the successive phrases of the work, pulling back for this one, driving that one forward. The very plasticity of the tempo-modification suggests that the tradition of which he is a part conceives the interpretative task more as one of bringing to life and nurturing a constantly changing organism than as one of managing a series of events that might be properly clocked with a metronome. And despite some ragged playing from the London Symphony Orchestra – most notably at the end of the first movement, which the orchestra's members finish at different times – Kajanus's recording helps us to understand Sibelius's own caveats with regard to his metronome markings of the early 1940s.

It would appear that the slow-to-fast motion of the first movement has led several subsequent conductors to play its opening at slower tempos than Sibelius would have preferred to hear. Kajanus's pre-scherzo portion is one of the fastest recorded, but it is generally consistent with the composer's indications in Table 1. Even Maazel's opening, at 54 – the onset of an unusually brisk, coolly ordered reading – is considerably slower than Kajanus's. Apparently as a corrective move, several conductors then accelerate the tempo toward the end of the first rotation (that is, at least with the onset of the 'closing theme' at letter I, bar 62) in order to cycle more rapidly through the second rotation. Sibelius himself, however, seems to have implied that, notwithstanding the generally flexible pulse, no such *più mosso* should occur until (one presumes) the approach to the climactic breakthrough after the *Largamente*. Here again Kajanus's recording is exemplary. Davis and Karajan, too, conduct the first two rotations at about the same speed, but since in these cases the first-rotation tempo was slow to begin with, the deliberate (and relatively rubato-free) performance of the more active second rotation creates an uncanny, 'ritualistic' effect.

Perhaps the most surprising feature of Kajanus's first movement is the rapid pace of its climactic 'B-major' breakthrough (bar 106), much faster than that of its successors and double the speed of Karajan and Bernstein at this point: this may be an important feature of the work's original tradition that has been lost.[15] Kajanus's speed permits him to glide smoothly into the scherzo at 88, slightly faster than Sibelius's suggestion of 80, to which he then drops back at the return to the three-flat signature at bar 158. Most of the other conductors in Table 2 begin the scherzo too slowly, by Sibelius's norms, and their *accelerando* progress through the movement may be readily compared with that suggested in Table 1. In terms of tempo Kajanus's and, especially, Ashkenazy's scherzos are probably the closest to Sibelius's indications. After a rapid *stringendo* out of the slow breakthrough, for example, Ashkenazy begins it precisely at the composer's preferred speed, but we might notice that he activates the *poco a poco stretto* a bit too soon. Bernstein's scherzo, on the other hand, is so astonishingly slow that it leaves the interpretative tradition behind to become a floating dreamscape or a private, contemplative meditation on the passing *Klänge*.

Sibelius's single indication of 80 for the middle movement is, of course, inadequate to describe a complex series of sound-events that is subjected to many tempo changes indicated in the score itself, at least from bar 70 onward (*rallent. al . . . Poco tranquillo*). Nonetheless, as a general marking it again suggests that the tendency has been to pace the movement more slowly than he might have liked. It would seem that even Kajanus was too deliberate for Sibelius here – at least up to the point of the second rotation – and it may be that of the performances cited in Table 2 Karajan's or Berglund's recording gives us the clearest image of the composer's intended pace. (Though probably too rapid, Maazel's is also instructive in this regard, once past the introduction.) It might be added, however, that perhaps another clear – and somewhat authoritative – sense of this movement's tempo may be obtained from Koussevitzky's 1940 recording with the Boston Symphony Orchestra: he begins the movement at c. 66 and gradually accelerates the pulse; by rotation 1 and the pizzicato theme (bar 14ff) it is perfectly on track, c. 76–80.

On the other hand, for the finale – another movement with several explicit tempo changes toward its end – Sibelius's general marking of 160 is actually slower than any of the performances charted in Table 2, although Kajanus's, Karajan's, Berglund's, and Bernstein's tempos, surely, are eminently within range. In most of these performances the conductors relax the pace to expand at the Swan Hymn: Kajanus and Ashkenazy provide the greatest tempo contrast here, and it may be that the nineteenth-century practice of slowing down for more expansive or lyrical 'second themes' is perfectly appropriate at this point. Sibelius himself left us with no advice on the matter, and we might note both that Karajan holds virtually to the same tempo here and that – surprisingly – Berglund alone actually conducts the second theme at a slightly faster speed than that of the first.

None of this is to suggest that tempos alone make or break a performance. In the case of the Fifth Symphony many other features also loom large: the 'phenomenological' contemplation of *Klang* (Karajan and Bernstein are particularly notable here), orchestral balance, the shaping and articulation of phrases, style and tone, the bringing forth of important motive- and timbre-anticipations of future events, providing a suitable heft and bite at climactic passages, and so on. Moreover, it is also clear that merely to measure tempos with a metronomic probe and then to presume to pronounce authoritatively on a performance's 'correctness' is a practice that degenerates all too rapidly into non-musical mindlessness.

In short, the tempo observations above are to be taken merely descriptively, not evaluatively. By the end of the twentieth century, one might hope, we have moved beyond the argument that a musical work's potential 'meaning' is to be limited either to a sonic imitation of certain external features of its original acoustic surface or to a musicologically reconstructed vision of that most intangible of intangibles, its composer's 'original intention'. The *de facto* interpretative tradition has certain claims as well – what a work has 'come to mean' in the history that reaches down to us. In any event it is questionable whether any tradition, even one so brief as that of the recorded interpretations of the Fifth Symphony, may be so easily leaped over – with the pretence of erasing it – in the expectation of being able to recover a presumably 'more authentic' practice. Old worlds are not so simplistically recaptured. They are enormously complex, socially grounded discourse systems of production- and reception-conventions. And they consist of elements far more central than measurably 'proper' tempos.

The principal desideratum, it would seem, is that interpretative decisions be made deliberately and consciously. They are to be made with all the facts in, not in ignorance of the differing options and the various authorities that they represent. But, in the end, it seems probable that the 'real' Fifth Symphony, in its original social and historical fullness – situated naturally in the discourse network of its own times, 'as it really was' – has now receded out of the grasp of our very different world. It can never be adequately, much less fully, recovered.

Notes

Preface

1 Quoted in Cherniavsky, 'Sibelius's tempo corrections', p. 53.
2 It is worth underscoring further the centrality of Tawaststjerna's achievement: it is nothing short of the crucial 'bottom-line' of present-day Sibelius scholarship. Because of the inaccessibility of such things as most of the original correspondence and the extremely important diaries, now sequestered in Finland's State Archives in Helsinki, the printed and Finnish-translated volumes of Tawaststjerna, who had access to all of these things, remain our principal source for basic data, including especially letter and diary transcriptions and precise dating. Any serious work on Sibelius today is nearly totally dependent on them. (It might be added that a few diary entries not included in Tawaststjerna may be found – in Italian – in Tammaro, *Le sinfonie di Sibelius* and in his related *Jean Sibelius*.)
3 Gray, *Sibelius*, p. 187.
4 Adorno, *Introduction*, p. 172. Adorno also reported (p. 173) that Ernest Newman's reply to this charge was that these qualities 'were just what appealed to the British'. Cf. Adorno's bitterest attack on the composer, 'Glosse über Sibelius', and Tawaststjerna's much later response to it, 'Über Adornos Sibelius-Kritik'.

1 Introduction

1 Lambert, *Music Ho!*, p. 323.
2 Dahlhaus, *Nineteenth-Century Music*, p. 367. For Adorno, see the 'Preface', n. 4, above.
3 On this perennial issue the most reliable source in English at the time of this writing is Tawaststjerna, 'Sibelius's Eighth Symphony' Cf. also, however, the scattered references to the Eighth in Tawaststjerna, *Jean Sibelius*, V.
4 Dahlhaus, *Nineteenth-Century Music*, pp. 330, 334.
5 Merian, *Richard Strauss' Tondichtung, Also sprach Zarathustra: Eine Studie über die moderne Programmsymphonie* (Leipzig: Carl Meyer, 1899), pp. 8–10; Oscar Bie, *Die moderne Musik und Richard Strauss* (Berlin: Bard Marquardt [1906]), p. 26.
6 Adapted principally from Bürger and Hohendahl, this sense of 'institution' refers to the complex social and economic network that within any society – but especially within 'modern' commercial societies – makes the concept of 'art' possible and sets the terms of its apprehension. To consider such an institution is to ask pointed questions about 'the function of art in its social contingency . . . [or about an artwork's] relationship to the *material conditions of the production and reception of art*' (Bürger, 'The institution of "art"', pp. 7–8; cf., for example, Hohendahl, 'Introduction' to *Building a National Literature*).
7 Needless to say, the case for the Bavarian Strauss as an unquestioned 'insider' is clearer than that for the Austrian-Jewish Mahler, whose ethnic background emerges often as a decidedly unpleasant bone of contention among certain writers of this period. See, for example, the playing of the racial card against Mahler by the Strauss partisan Rudolf Louis in *Die deutsche Musik der Gegenwart* (Munich and Leipzig: Georg Müller, 1909), pp. 180–85. See also Henry A. Lea's recent treatment of this aspect of Mahler and his world in *Gustav Mahler: Man on the Margin* (Bonn: Bouvier, 1985; cf. its review by John Williamson, *Music & Letters*, 67 (1986),

309–10). Notwithstanding these very real, disturbing undercurrents, the essential argument may still be pursued that, as a whole, the contemporary Austro-Germanic 'institution of art music' regarded Mahler as a major force. What is needed, of course, is a broader, dispassionate study of the cultural and ethnic politics within the larger institution of art music around the turn of the century – and of the degree to which such politics helped to shape the styles, social system-networks, and history of that music.

8 Niemann, *Jean Sibelius*, pp. 47–9. Niemann's influential misreadings of Sibelius's symphonies began around 1906 with his *Die Musik Skandinaviens*: see Tawaststjerna (trans. Layton), *Sibelius*, II, 52–3.

9 Hepokoski, 'Fiery-pulsed libertine'.

10 See the discussion in ibid., which is also indebted to concepts of Theodor W. Adorno and Bernd Sponheuer. It might be added that an allied variant of the normal 'developmental' or 'onset-of-recapitulation' breakthrough is the 'coda' breakthrough, featuring essentially new, 'redemptive' material that emerges only after a sonata (or a deformation thereof) has been completed. Some classic early examples include Beethoven's *Egmont* Overture and the finale of Mendelssohn's 'Scottish' Symphony. Cf. also n.17 below.

11 With its central, developmental-space episode and reversed order of themes in the recapitulatory space, Wagner's overture is also designed to suggest an expansive arch. (Some aspects of this sonata deformation, including the emphatically recurring introduction, may have been modelled on certain features of Berlioz's overtures – for instance, *Les franc-juges* and *Benvenuto Cellini*. See Julian Rushton's discussion of these and other Berlioz pieces, n. 13 below.) Nevertheless the principal generic tradition within which the *Tannhäuser* Overture is clearly situated, and to which its deformational procedures ultimately allude, is that of the sonata-based operatic overture with slow introduction.

12 Cf. also the precedent in such works as the first movement of Beethoven's *Pathétique* Sonata.

13 In *Les franc-juges* at least one extensive developmental-space episode is clear; see the argument on behalf of a second in Julian Rushton, *The Musical Language of Berlioz* (Cambridge: Cambridge University Press, 1983), pp. 191–2. Rushton's general discussion of Berlioz's unusual structures in his instrumental works (pp. 181–227) is highly relevant to the concept of 'deformation' proposed above. Also central to the whole question are Thomas S. Grey, 'Wagner, the overture, and the aesthetics of musical form', *19th-Century Music*, 12 (1988), 3–22; and Michael Tusa, *Euryanthe and Carl Maria von Weber's Dramaturgy of German Opera* (Oxford: Clarendon, 1991), pp. 27–30, 249–76.

14 This type is considered further in Hepokoski, 'Structure and program in *Macbeth*'.

15 Cf. the mention of Berliozian strophes in Rushton, *The Musical Language of Berlioz*, e.g., pp. 196–7. I use the term 'carnivalesque' here primarily in the well-known sense of Mikhail Bakhtin, *Rabelais and His World*, trans. Helene Iswolsky (Cambridge, Mass.: MIT Press, 1968, also 1971).

16 See, for example, Carl Dahlhaus, *Richard Wagner's Music Dramas*, trans. Mary Whittall (Cambridge: Cambridge University Press, 1979), p. 71. Cf. Dahlhaus on Liszt and others, *Nineteenth-Century Music*, pp. 236–44, 360–68.

17 Tailored somewhat to the ensuing Sibelius discussion, the list, of course, makes no claim to completeness. Among some other procedures are: the well-known Brahmsian Deformation within works with non-repeated expositions (see, for example, the discussion in Robert Pascall, 'Some special uses of sonata form by Brahms', *Soundings*, 4 (1974), 58–63) – a deformation apparently associated with 'conservative' composition; the Brucknerian Deformation, which may have broad affinities with 'rotational' or 'strophic-sonata' hybrids; and the deformation of the 'non-resolving recapitulation', in which a sonata's 'second theme' (or any theme that is used to bring the exposition to a non-tonic close) is not permitted to resolve satisfactorily to the presumed 'tonic' in the recapitulatory space, thus creating a sense of unease, alienation, futility, recapitulatory failure, or the like. (In this last case the anticipated 'tonic' resolution, though dramatically delayed, is normally accomplished – whether redemptively, playfully, or

tragically – in a special coda space as in Beethoven's *Egmont* Overture, Glinka's Overture to *Russian and Ludmilla*, and Tchaikovsky's *Romeo and Juliet*. Cf. the masterly treatment of key and structure in the first, third, and fourth movements of Elgar's First Symphony, which concern themselves with sophisticated variants of this and other deformations.)

18 Dahlhaus, *Nineteenth-Century Music*, p. 336.

2 The crisis

1 For example, the issue of the restoration of an architectonic rigour whose new forms might harness the power of modern 'colouristic' content was very much in the Berlin air in 1905, precisely as Sibelius was conducting his 'modern' Second Symphony there. Particularly telling in this regard is the conclusion of Karl Schmalz's essay, 'Richard Strauss' "Also sprach Zarathustra" und "Ein Heldenleben": ein Vergleich', in the widely read Berlin periodical *Die Musik*, 4 (1904–5), 102–23, which touches on the controversy over Strauss's recent *Symphonia domestica*. As a self-proclaimed partisan of *Zarathustra* Schmalz calls here for a new, redefined classicism: 'not a turning-back [*Umkehr*] in the reactionary sense, in the sense of the historic forms . . . [but one that makes modern use of] the musical material of today, yes – and in new forms; but again, in such a way that form and content are brought into balance' (p. 122). Using essentially the same words four years later, Rudolf Louis expanded this argument in the opening essay in *Die deutsche Musik der Gegenwart* (Munich and Leipzig: Müller, 1909), which after a broad discussion concludes with the ringing slogan, 'Reaction not as a turning-back [*Umkehr*], rather: reaction as progress [*Fortschritt*]'.

2 To what extent Sibelius's private conversations with his friend Busoni at this time also played a role in all of this is currently unclear, although one suspects that their impact might have been profound. It is worth remarking, though, that, as Antony Beaumont demonstrated in a paper, 'Sibelius and Busoni', delivered at the 23–5 August 1990 Sibelius Conference in Helsinki, Busoni's concept of *junge Klassizität* proper was developed only toward the end of the 1910s (*pace* Tawaststjerna(trans. Layton), vol.II, pp. 26, 67, 116, etc.). Cf. Busoni's more 'radical' concerns in the 1906–15 years, discussed in Beaumont, *Busoni the Composer* (Bloomington: Indiana University Press, 1985), pp. 89–203. And cf. chapter 3 below, n. 2.

3 These and all subsequent parenthetical references in the text are to Tawaststjerna's multivolume, Finnish-language biography, *Jean Sibelius*. Vols. I–III, however, have also appeared in Robert Layton's slightly abbreviated *two*-volume English translation (from the original Swedish), *Sibelius*, to which the reader might find it more convenient to refer (see the 'Preface' above and the 'Select Bibliography' below.) Cross-references to the *corresponding* passage in the Layton volumes are indicated with an asterisk. Note: I have often altered or amplified the Layton translation on the basis of the printed Finnish text. While my translations retain Layton's as a base, then, the citations to the English edition typically do not quote verbatim from it. All of the provided dates – frequently omitted in the English translation – are taken from the fuller, Finnish-language edition.

4 Cf. Sibelius on Mahler, in an interview with Leevi Madetoja printed in the *Helsingin Sanomat* on 10 August 1916: 'That being composed today is already old tomorrow. By now Mahler's symphonies, which only a few years ago were believed to be totally innovative, have already lost almost all of their meaning in that sense. As for me, I find nothing more in them than worn-out sentimental thoughts'. (IV, 177) Cf. Sibelius on Schoenberg in the same interview, n. 13 below.

5 Tawaststjerna (Layton), *Sibelius*, *II, 139.

6 Cf., though, the prominent open fifths in one of Sibelius's works of the next few years, *The Bard* (1913, rev. 1914), 1–3 bars before letter K.

7 Newmarch, *Jean Sibelius*, pp. 35–6.

8 Levas, *Sibelius*, p. 74. 'I was one of the first to get hold of Arnold Schoenberg's works for himself. I bought them on Busoni's advice, to learn something. But I learned nothing.'

9 This important letter has been printed – in Italian translation – in Tammaro, *Le sinfonie*, pp. 159–60, with the dating given on p. 164. (It might be added as a point of caution that Tammaro's book elsewhere contains a few errors of dating and translation.) Tawaststjerna does not include the letter in his biography.

10 Reginald Pound, *Sir Henry Wood* (London: Cassell, 1969), p. 118.

11 For Sibelius on Scriabin, see Newmarch, *Jean Sibelius*, pp. 48–9; cf. Tawaststjerna, *Sibelius*, IV, 17–18.

12 It might be observed that the sentence 'They see me . . .' appears in two contradictory translations in III, 318 (the original Swedish translated into Finnish) and *II, 240 ('They don't see me. . . .'). That in III, 318, makes more contextual sense and has been used here.

13 Cf. Sibelius's remarks on Schoenberg in the 1916 interview with Madetoja (see n. 4 above): 'Despite all their "revolutionary quality", Schoenberg's *Gurrelieder*, which I have just been leafing through, are orchestrated at rather a beginning student's level'. (IV, 177) The key to understanding this remark lies in grasping Sibelius's sense of elemental *Klang*. See chapter 3, pp. 27–9, below.

3 Reassessed compositional principles

1 Both quotations are from Tammaro, *Le sinfonie*, p. 139.

2 For the parenthetical, abbreviated citation form within the text see above, chapter 2, n. 3. (Cf. the translation in Tammaro, *Le sinfonie*, p. 139.) It may be important also to note the same idea in two of Busoni's letters to Robert Freund, 25 April 1907 ('I am not speaking of formlessness but rather of traditional forms, which should be cast off, and I maintain that every new idea calls for a new structure') and 8 November 1910 ('But I reject *traditional* and *unalterable* forms and feel that every idea, every motif, every object demands its *own* form, related to that idea, to that motif, to that object'), in Antony Beaumont, *Ferruccio Busoni: Selected Letters* (New York: Columbia University Press, 1987), pp. 84–5, 114–15. Busoni's letters were called to the attention of Sibelians by Beaumont in his paper at the 1990 Sibelius Conference; see chapter 2, n. 2 above.

3 Tammaro, *Le sinfonie*, p. 139. Dating from Tammaro, *Jean Sibelius* (Turin: ERI, Edizione RAI, 1984), p. 372, n. 6. In both books Tammaro also cites the first volume of Tawaststjerna, *Sibelius*, Swedish edition (1968), I, 13. The quotation, it seems, does not appear in the Finnish-language edition.

4 Marx, *Die Lehre von der musikalischen Komposition*, 4th edn (Leipzig: Breitkopf & Härtel, 1868), III, 335–40. The quotations are taken from p. 336. For Sibelius's early grounding in this work, and in Marx's formal systems, see Tawaststjerna (trans. Layton), *Sibelius*, *I, 22.

5 Levas, *Sibelius*, pp. 82–3.

6 Cf. the discussion of the *telos* principle in Strauss's *Don Juan*, in Hepokoski, 'Fiery-pulsed libertine'.

7 The qualification 'metaphorical' must appear here, because the emergence of the natural world at the end of Sibelius's *Luonnotar* – a work that may be considered to illustrate the core of Sibelius's aesthetic – results not from the anticipated human birth process but from the incubating and cracking of a primal 'cosmic egg'. In the complete story, found in Runo 1 of the *Kalevala*, the 'literal' pregnancy of the 'Feminine Nature Spirit' (or the 'Luonnotar') – which also plays an important role in Sibelius's work – leads, at the end of the Runo (after the appearance of the world out of the bird's egg), to the strained birth of the godlike Väinömöinen. By choosing to set only a selection of verses from the original poem, Sibelius, in effect, suggests a fusion of the two differing creation stories in the *Kalevala* – the painfully burdensome pregnancy of Ilmatar (the 'Luonnotar') and her simultaneous incubation of the cosmic egg – into a single myth. As an implicitly 'closed' tale, Sibelius's setting seems to encourage the implication by metaphor that this 'Luonnotar' has, in fact, given birth to the world. Confronting this aspect of *Luonnotar* (which also involves comparing it with the various

versions of the poems from which the *Kalevala* was shaped) is extraordinarily complex and raises a number of gender-related issues, several of which I treat in my essay on that work in *The Sibelius Companion*, ed. Glenda Dawn Goss (New York: Greenwood, forthcoming in 1993).

8 Heidegger, 'The origin of the work of art', in *Poetry, Language, Thought*, trans. Albert Hofstadter (New York: Harper & Row, 1971), pp. 51, 59.

9 See, for example, the discussion of nineteenth-century *Klang* and *Klangfläche* in Dahlhaus, *Nineteenth-Century Music*, pp. 306–11.

10 De Törne, *Sibelius*, p. 97. On Sibelius's orchestration and its underlying aesthetic cf. de Törne, pp. 29–39, 53–6, 89–92, 95–6, and Levas, *Sibelius*, pp. 36–9, 46–7, 88–9.

11 It is not a rondo, as is sometimes remarked, although its rotational form is easily taken for the rondo principle, as in Howell, *Jean Sibelius*, pp. 254–5. Sibelius's early title for it, 'Rondo of the Waves', better fits its little-known, unpublished (and rotational) second version – which has never been performed – than this third, final version. On the topic of prior discussions of *The Oceanides*, I might add that I find the label of 'impressionism', invariably associated with this piece, to be both misleading and without value. Sibelius's regard for *Klang* effects and structures is evident throughout his entire career. We need not appeal to 'Debussyism' to account for it.

12 See, for example, Dahlhaus, *Nineteenth-Century Music*, pp. 135–7, 236–44, 360–68; 'Liszt, Schönberg und die große Form: das Prinzip der Mehrsätzigkeit in der Einsätzigkeit', *Die Musikforschung*, 41 (1988), 202–13; Howell, *Jean Sibelius*, pp. 33–72; Hepokoski, 'Fiery-pulsed libertine' and 'Structure and program'. Cf. also the deformational processes mentioned in chapter 1 above.

13 Tawaststjerna (trans. Layton), *Sibelius*, *II, 24, 78.

4 Of Heaven's door and migrating swans

1 The relevant orchestral sketch, written on the outside page of a bifolio of 18-stave paper – and numbered A/0335 in Kilpeläinen, *The Jean Sibelius Musical Manuscripts* – consists of about fifteen bars in a rudimentary score format. Its bars 7–15 are essentially equivalent to 8–15 of Ex. 3 (bars 11 and 15 of Ex. 3 are held for two bars; 14 is omitted). Its opening, however, differs slightly: bar 1 contains only a tremolo 'E♭⁶' chord in the upper strings; mm. 2–6 consist of an elemental, slow call-and-response in the horns, the linear open fifth e♭¹–b♭¹ (2–4) overlapped and answered by a slow, dotted-rhythm e♭¹–f¹–b♭¹ (4–6). This sketch is idiosyncratic among the Fifth Symphony collection as gathered in the Helsinki University Library, and it is generally in the vicinity of materials that would seem to date no earlier than 1916. The inner pages of the same bifolio, for example, are concerned with creating the opening of the 1916 or 1919 version. It may be, then, that Sibelius returned to this 'initial' idea quite late, even after he had already once discarded it for use in the Fifth Symphony: cf. the discussion below of Sibelius's plan for a radical revision of the work in early 1918. On the other hand, it may also be that the E♭ sketch on the first page of the bifolio was actually for a different work, although at present this seems unlikely.

2 Tawaststjerna, *Jean Sibelius*, IV, 58 mistakenly includes Ex. 2β in the first movement.

3 Trans. partially based on that of William Moore, notes (by Hannu-Ilari Lampila) for the Paavo Berglund recording of the Fifth, EMI 7 49175 2, released in 1988.

4 Cf. Sibelius's diary entry from nearly four years earlier, 5 November 1911: 'A symphony is not just a composition in the ordinary sense of the word; it is more of an inner confession at a given stage of one's life.' (III, 215; *II, 159)

5 For more on Sibelius's fascination with the Järvenpää swans and other spring- and fall-migrating birds, see De Törne, *Sibelius*, p. 101, and Levas, *Sibelius*, p. 49, in which Sibelius is said to have described the call of the crane as 'the *Leitmotiv* of my life'. Cf. n. 12 below.

6 The (undated) sketch transcribed in Ex. 7 is on the sketch-page numbered A/0359 in

Kilpeläinen, *The Jean Sibelius Musical Manuscripts*. The connection between the Fifth's sketched Adagio theme and the theme of the Seventh is also drawn in the excellent study by Kari Kilpeläinen, 'Jean Sibeliuksen 7. sinfonian musiikillisista lähteistä ja teoksen synnystä niiden valossa' ('The musical sources for Jean Sibelius's 7th Symphony and the birth of the work as seen in their light'). This essay, edited and translated by the present author, will appear under the title 'Sibelius's Seventh Symphony: an introduction to the manuscript and printed sources' in the forthcoming *The Sibelius Companion*, ed. Glenda Dawn Goss (Westport, Connecticut: Greenwood). Among Sibelius's sketches for the Seventh Symphony there exist many – dozens – of variants of this melody and of melodies in what Kilpeläinen calls its 'family'. Kilpeläinen, who had access not only to more pages of the 1914–15 sketchbook than were reproduced in Tawaststjerna, IV, but also to the complete collection of sketches in the Helsinki University Library, transcribes several of them and points out that in some of its earlier phases this 'Seventh Symphony' melody appears in D major. In this key it seems at one point to have been planned as part of the never-completed symphonic poem, *Kuutar* ([Feminine-] Moon-Spirit), perhaps, as one of the *Kuutar* theme-tables suggests, of the section provisionally titled 'Tähtölä' ('Where the Stars Dwell'). Only in the 1920s was the theme transposed to C major.

7 The transcription of a number of these examples differs from that provided in Tawaststjerna, *Jean Sibelius*, IV, 54–74, an important discussion of the sketchbook material. In this instance, on IV, 63, Tawaststjerna transcribed the second note of bar 4 as a d^1, although, to judge from the photograph of the sketch provided four plates before p. 177, it seems clearly to be an e^1. Similarly, Tawaststjerna omits a (seemingly redundant) duplication of four pitches, beginning at the end of bar 7; and he adds clarifying barlines after bar 7. It might be added that the music continues for another phrase or two beyond that provided in Ex.9: this continuation unmistakably anticipates the goal-variant of the theme as heard at the end of the 1915 version (see pp. 47–9 above). Sibelius suppressed this variant ending in the familiar, 1919 version.

8 Given its initial placement in Tawaststjerna's book, the date of 2 October seems most likely, but on IV, 25 Tawaststjerna (mistakenly?) refers back to this diary entry as belonging to 2 November.

9 The programme is reproduced in Parmet, *The Symphonies*, p. 69; see also Dahlström, *The Works of Jean Sibelius*, p. 28. For the designations on the parts, see Kilpeläinen, *The Jean Sibelius Musical Manuscripts*, p. 58.

10 For example, in Pike, *Beethoven, Sibelius*, pp. 131–3; Simpson, *Carl Nielsen*, pp. 207–13; and, later, Howell, *Jean Sibelius*, pp. 43–5.

11 See n. 1 above.

12 Levas, *Sibelius*, p. xxii.

5 Musical process and architecture

1 Abraham, 'The symphonies', pp. 32–3.

2 See especially Howell, *Jean Sibelius*, p. 33.

3 Ringbom, *Jean Sibelius*, pp. 137–8; Parmet, *The Symphonies*, pp. 71–2; Simpson, *Carl Nielsen*, pp. 208–9.

4 See, for example, the differing proposals for the onset of the recapitulation in Tanzberger, *Jean Sibelius*, p. 114 (bar 106, the *fortissimo* shift to 'B major'); Layton, *Sibelius*, p. 50 (bar 158, the return to E♭); Tawaststjerna, *Jean Sibelius*, IV, 378–9, probably based on Abraham, 'The symphonies', p. 30 (bar 298, the return in scherzo guise of the exposition's second theme).

5 Compare also the opening intervals, 5̂–8̂–2̂ 5̂–3̂–1̂, of the second movement of Brahms's Double Concerto.

6 But note such prominent 'four-rotation' canonic models (unrepeated, multithematic exposition / development / recapitulation / coda) as the first movement of Beethoven's *Appassionata* Sonata and the finale of Mendelssohn's 'Scottish' Symphony. See chapter 1, p. 7 above.

7 For a closer harmonic analysis of this important, but non-cadential move into this 'B major', see Hepokoski, 'Structural tensions'.

8   The reading given here, of course, is that of the 1919 version (whose essential features at this point are also those of the 1916 version). The original, 1915 version, whose second movement began here after a pause, would demand a different reading of these events, one considerably less in dialogue with the expectations of sonata-deformational procedures. See chapter 4 above, 'The 1915 version'.

9   Parmet, *The Symphonies*, p. 76; Abraham, 'The symphonies', p. 30; Simpson, *Carl Nielsen*, p. 211; Layton, *Sibelius*, p. 51.

10 Theme and variations: Roiha, *Die Symphonien*, pp. 51–2, 123–5; Abraham, 'The symphonies', p. 30; Ringbom, *Jean Sibelius*, p. 138; Parmet, *The Symphonies*, p. 76; Layton, *Sibelius*, p. 51. *ABA*: Tawaststjerna, *Jean Sibelius*, IV, 363–7; cf. Simpson, *Carl Nielsen*, p. 211. Strophes: Tanzberger, *Jean Sibelius*, pp. 117–19.

11 The comparative Ex. 20 is adapted from Parmet, *The Symphonies*, p. 78. Although several writers have mentioned this point, none have gone beyond merely noting the resemblance between the two themes or suggesting, as in Layton, *Sibelius*, p. 51, that the passage merely 'hints' at the finale theme. This crucial resemblance was first mentioned in print by Ringbom, *Jean Sibelius*, p. 139n. According to Parmet, though, it was first pointed out by Jussi Jalas, the composer's son-in-law. Parmet went on to report, 'When questioned about this resemblance Sibelius emphasized the fact that it was a pure coincidence, and said that he had been quite unaware of the similarity between these two passages. He has reacted . . . in the same way concerning other thematic relations and resemblances which some scholars have pointed to in the symphonies' (pp. 78–9). Once one knows the compositional history of this movement, however, it is clear that Sibelius's disavowals were disingenuous, crafted to serve the myth of intuitive inspiration that he wished to make a central feature of his own mystique.

12 The format of this example is adapted from Tanzberger, *Jean Sibelius*, p. 117; it is also reproduced in Salmenhaara, *Jean Sibelius*, p. 362. The subsequent designations α and β, however, are my own.

13 For the passage in question see Tawaststjerna (trans. Layton), *Sibelius*, *II, 91, Ex. 49.

14 Undated sketch: numbered A/0339 in Kilpeläinen, *The Jean Sibelius Musical Manuscripts*, the transcription omits some discarded alternatives. A large part of the surviving sketch materials for the Fifth in the Helsinki University collection concerns this movement; most of these sketches seem to be rather late, from the post-1915 – and possibly post-1916 – revision periods. As mentioned above, it is only in the 1919 version that Sibelius chose to make this bass counterpoint explicit, although it was obviously implied in the earlier versions: perhaps this is the sketch's *raison d'être*. The treble melody in A/0339 is not found in exactly this way in any version: it seems to blend portions of the 1915 opening (bars 6ff) with aspects of what we are calling 'rotation 5'.

15 It may be remembered that the 1915 version of this movement began here with this woodwind swaying. See p. 47 above.

16 Pike, *Beethoven, Sibelius*, p. 131; cf. Pike, p. 135; Simpson, *Carl Nielsen*, p. 212; and Murtomäki, 'Sibelius symphoniste', p. 20, who writes about the 'symmetrical construction of the symphony'.

17 Abraham, 'The Symphonies', p. 30.

18 Parmet, *The Symphonies*, p. 81. Parmet's subsequent discussion does little to clarify his claim. His scheme would seem to suggest that the 'main theme' returns in bar 280, but elsewhere (p. 85) he implied that the 'working-out section' extended to bar 406. He then dubbed the problematic *Un pochettino largamente* an 'epilogue' (with pre-coda features) and, as usual, considered the 'coda' proper to begin at bar 427, the *Largamente assai*. Apparently he reckoned the return of the grand second theme in the 'coda' as the feature that defined the whole as a rondo – as opposed to a sonata. But if this is the case, of course, the section would not be a coda.

19 Tawaststjerna, *Jean Sibelius*, IV, 367, 369.

20 Tanzberger, *Jean Sibelius*, pp. 119–22.

21 See, for example, De Törne, *Sibelius*, pp. 30–31.
22 Moreover, the section is manifestly parallel both to the first movement's *Largamente*, bar 92, which had been the corridor leading to the 'B major' breakthrough, and to the slow movement's 'lake of tears' rotation 7.
23 Tawaststjerna, *Jean Sibelius*, IV, 371.

6 Editions and performance tempos

1 I am grateful to Professor Dahlström, who provided me with the editorial information that follows.
2 Levas, *Sibelius*, pp. 89–90.
3 Numbered A/1789 in Kilpeläinen, *The Jean Sibelius Musical Manuscripts*, p. 42.
4 Cherniavsky, 'Sibelius's tempo corrections', p. 54.
5 HMV Society Set 1, DB1739–42. It has subsequently been reissued both on LP and on compact disc.
6 Deutsche Grammophon SLPM 138973.
7 Decca SXL 6236, in the USA London CS 9488.
8 Philips 420 013–1.
9 Decca SXDL 7541, in the USA London LDR 71041.
10 Compact disc, EMI 7 49175 2.
11 Compact disc, Deutsche Grammophon 427 647–2.
12 With the Boston Symphony: HMV Album Series 337; in the USA Victor Masterworks Set 474; now available on compact disc, Pearl, GEMM CDS 9408.
13 Thomas, *The Symphonies*, is a useful discography of all the Sibelius symphonies through 1989 – I have used it extensively here – and it also provides a lively discussion and personal evaluation of their features (one, however, that seems unaware of Sibelius's metronome markings). Thomas lists forty-two recordings of the work from Kajanus through Berglund.
14 Thomas, *The Symphonies*, pp. 8, 30.
15 It is always difficult, of course, to generalize about a presumed tradition on the basis of a single recording. Koussevitzky's important 1940 reading with the Boston Symphony Orchestra begins the movement at c. 52 (by bars 3ff); his second rotation is somewhat faster, at c. 60–3; the 'B–major' breakthrough arrives at c. 64–6, with little *accelerando* into the *Allegro moderato*, which begins at c. 69.

Select bibliography

Abraham, Gerald. 'The symphonies', in *The Music of Sibelius*, ed. Gerald Abraham (New York: Norton, 1947), pp. 14–37

Adorno, Theodor W. 'Glosse über Sibelius', reprinted as part of the *Impromptus*, in *Gesammelte Schriften*, 17 (*Musikalische Schriften IV*), (Frankfurt: Suhrkamp, 1982), pp. 247–52; first publ. 1938 (in German)

Introduction to the Sociology of Music, trans. E. B. Ashton (New York: Continuum, 1989); first publ. 1962 (in German)

Berglund, Paavo. *A Comparative Study of the Printed Score and the Manuscript of the Seventh Symphony of Sibelius*, Acta Musica V, Studies Published by Sibelius Museum (Turku, 1970)

Preface to Sibelius, Symphony No. 5 for Orchestra, Op. 82 [orchestral score, rev. edn., No. 2086] (Copenhagen: Wilhelm Hansen, 1974)

Bürger, Peter. 'The institution of "art" as a category in the sociology of literature', *Cultural Critique*, 2 (1985–6), pp. 5–33; first publ. 1977 (in German)

Cherniavsky, David. 'Sibelius's tempo corrections', *Music & Letters*, 31 (1950), pp. 53–5 (see also 'Metronomimerkinnät')

Dahlhaus, Carl. *Nineteenth-Century Music*, trans. J. Bradford Robinson (Berkeley: University of California Press, 1989); first publ. 1980 (in German)

Dahlström, Fabian. *The Works of Jean Sibelius* (Helsinki: Sibelius Seura (Sibelius Society), 1987)

Gray, Cecil. *Sibelius*, 2nd edn (London: Oxford, 1931); first publ. 1931

Hepokoski, James. 'Fiery-pulsed libertine or domestic hero?: Strauss's *Don Juan* reinvestigated', in *Richard Strauss: New Perspectives on the Composer and His Works*, ed. Bryan Gilliam (Durham: Duke University Press, 1992), forthcoming

'Structural tensions in Sibelius's Fifth Symphony: notes on the dissolution of "Modernism"', forthcoming in the *Proceedings of the First International Sibelius Congress* (Helsinki, 23–5 April 1990), ed. Eero Tarasti (publication data currently lacking)

'Structure and program in *Macbeth*: a proposed reading of Strauss's first symphonic poem', in *Strauss and His World*, ed. Bryan Gilliam (Princeton: Princeton University Press, 1992), pp. 67–89

Hohendahl, Peter Uwe. *Building a National Literature: The Case of Germany, 1830–1870*, trans. Renate Baron Franciscono (Ithaca: Cornell University Press, 1989); first publ. 1985 (in German)

Howell, Tim. *Jean Sibelius: Progressive Techniques in the Symphonies and Tone Poems* (New York and London: Garland, 1989)

Jalas, Jussi. *Kirjoituksia Sibeliuksen sinfonioista: Sinfonian eettinen pakko* (Helsinki: Fazer, 1988)

Kilpeläinen, Kari. 'Jean Sibeliuksen 7. sinfonian musiikillisista lähteistä ja teoksen synnystä niiden valossa', *Musiikki*, 7 (1990), pp. 39–72

The Jean Sibelius Musical Manuscripts at Helsinki University Library: A Complete Catalogue (Wiesbaden: Breitkopf & Härtel, 1991)

Lambert, Constant. *Music Ho!: A Study of Music in Decline* (New York: Scribner's, 1934)

Layton, Robert. *Sibelius*, rev. edn (London: Dent, 1978)

Levas, Santeri. *Sibelius: A Personal Portrait*, trans. Percy M. Young (London: Dent, 1972)

'Metronomimerkinnät Sibeliuksen Sinfonioihin', *Musiikkitieto*, 1/1943, p. 12

Murtomäki, Veijo. 'Sibelius symphoniste', *Finnish Music Quarterly* (Numéro special en français) [1990], pp. 12–22

Newmarch, Rosa. *Jean Sibelius: A Short Story of a Long Friendship* (Boston: Birchard, 1934)

Niemann, Walter. *Jean Sibelius* (Leipzig: Breitkopf & Härtel, 1917)

Parmet, Simon. *The Symphonies of Sibelius: A Study in Musical Appreciation*, trans. Kingsley A. Hart (London: Cassell, 1959); first publ. 1955 (in Swedish)

Pike, Lionel. *Beethoven, Sibelius and the 'Profound Logic': Studies in Symphonic Analysis* (London: Athlone, 1978)

Ringbom, Nils-Eric. *Jean Sibelius: A Master and his Work*, trans. G. I. C. de Courcy (Norman: University of Oklahoma, 1954); first publ. 1948 (in Swedish)

Roiha, Eino. *Die Symphonien von Jean Sibelius: Eine Form-analytische Studie* (Jyväskylä: Gummerus, 1941)

Salmenhaara, Erkki. *Jean Sibelius* (Helsinki: Tammi, 1984) (in Finnish)

Simpson, Robert. *Carl Nielsen: Symphonist*, rev. edn (London: Kahn & Averill, 1979)

Tammaro, Ferruccio. *Jean Sibelius* (Turin: ERI/Edizioni RAI, 1984)

Le Sinfonie di Sibelius (Turin: Giappichelli, 1982)

Tanzberger, Ernst. *Jean Sibelius: Eine Monographie* (Wiesbaden: Breitkopf & Härtel, 1962)

Tawaststjerna, Erik. *Jean Sibelius*, 5 vols. (Helsinki: Otava, 1965–88; vol. 1, rev. 1989) (trans. into Finnish from the original Swedish by Tuomas Anhava, Raija Mattila, and Erkki Salmenhaara)

Sibelius (slightly abridged translation of vols. 1–3 of the above – from the original Swedish – by Robert Layton), 2 vols. (London: Faber and Faber, 1976, 1986; a third and final volume, encompassing the original vols. 4–5, is forthcoming)

'Sibelius's Eighth Symphony – an insoluble mystery', *Finnish Music Quarterly* (1985), pp. 61–70, 92–101

'Über Adornos Sibelius-Kritik', *Adorno und die Musik*, ed. Otto Kolleritsch (Graz: Universal Edition, 1979), pp. 112–24

Thomas, Guy. 'The Symphonies of Jean Sibelius: A Discography and Discussion' (Bloomington: Indiana University School of Music, Department of Audio, 1990, privately distributed by the publishers)

Törne, Bengt de. *Sibelius: A Close-Up* (Boston: Houghton Mifflin, 1938)

Vignal, Marc. *Jean Sibelius: l'homme et son oeuvre* (Paris: Seghers, 1965)

Index

Also of interest

Mahler: Symphony No. 3

Peter Franklin
Lecturer in Music,
University of Leeds

Mahler's Third Symphony was conceived as a musical picture of the natural world. This handbook describes the composition of Mahler's grandiose piece of philosophical programme music in the context of the ideas that inspired it and the artistic debates and social conflicts that it reflects. In this original and wide-ranging account, Peter Franklin takes the Third Symphony as a representative modern European symphony of its period and evaluates the piece as both the culmination of Mahler's early symphonic style and a work whose contradictory effects mirror the complexity of contemporary social and musical manners. The music is described in detail, movement by movement, with chapters on the genesis, early performance and subsequent reception of the work.